i'm
BACK

How to get your passion, purpose and identity back
when your kids go to school

JENNIE HK

www.90daybooks.com

First published in Great Britain in 2012 by 90-Day Books, a trading name of Meaningful Goals Ltd., Sussex, England. www.90daybooks.com

Author's photograph, cover design and layout by Michael Kopinski www.thetalentedstudio.com.

Book design and layout by Kevin Bermingham, 90-Day Books.

British Library Cataloguing in Publication Data.
A catalogue record for this book is available from the British Library.

V2-Paperback edition

ISBN 978-1-908101-10-5

1. Self-Improvement

My Gratitude

I have overwhelming gratitude, as ever, to my inspiring husband from whom I have learnt not to settle for mediocrity in any area of life

To my family who are as solid as they come, in particular to Mum, Dad and my beautiful sister for their relentless editing

To Michael Kopinski, a remarkable creative talent and gorgeous human being who created the cover from photography to design

(www.thetalentedstudio.com)

To Kevin Bermingham who kicked my butt and gave me the push I needed to write a book in 90 days

(www.90daybooks.com)

Some kind words

"Down to earth, friendly, feminine and relatable. A great read from start to finish. Jennie is very clear who this book is for. It is so well targeted that I was hooked from the start. Her honesty and humour is a breath of fresh air - so unlike any other motivational / self-help / change your life book. If you really are ready to remember who you are and take the first steps towards living an authentic, inspiring life you have got to get your teeth into this."

Katie Phillips

Founder, www.daringandmighty.com

Contents

Introduction

"Life should NOT be a journey to the grave with the intention of arriving safely in an attractive well preserved body, but rather skid in sideways, chocolate in one hand, champagne in the other, body thoroughly used up, totally worn out"

If I was to ask you what a fish, a tantrum and front crawl had to do with getting your mojo back in life you would understandably be a little bemused. Life is funny like that; it often throws up obscure events that turn out to be some of our most defining moments.

This book has been born out of some of my 'moments' over the last few years, and as random as they may seem, they really have had such an impact on me that the landscape of my future was literally altered overnight.

I decided to sit down and share these experiences because of the value they can bring to you, if understood in the right context and acted upon. Before I begin though, let's get clear on whom this book is for and who it isn't, as we are busy people and I don't want to waste your time.

If you are perfectly happy with the way things are at the moment, you only have a mild interest in getting out there and mixing things up and you don't want to rock the boat, then this book probably isn't for you right now.

However, if you have become aware of a voice inside of you urging you to grow in some respect, in fact, it is screaming at you and you can't ignore it any more, then you are in the right place.

This is not a book about how to have it all or attain a perfect life balance because quite frankly I think that is deluded. Life is full of compromises and there are going to be times as a mother that, if you take on this work, you are going to be juggling like a lunatic. The difference though, is that you will feel ALIVE.

Through applying the information in this book you can discover what it is that is going to get you jumping out of bed in the morning raring to go, both in your role as a mother and in your role of being you. Feeling inspired by life and inspired by what you are up to in the world is one of the best feelings in the world. This is my want for you.

I am going to ask you to park those thoughts that may already be penetrating your mind about time constraints, financial constraints, and any other circumstantial restraints, including the 'it's alright for you' thoughts that you may be having right now. We'll tackle those throughout the book.

If you live your life day by day, reacting to whatever is thrown up for you for the next forty years, before you know it you will be reflecting back wondering what happened to all those missed opportunities. Don't be that person.

Your life is happening now. With kids at school or heading to school this stage in life is priceless. You could be experiencing, achieving, contributing and adding value to others beyond what you can even comprehend right now.

I am excited to share with you how I discovered what it was that I wanted to do, and how that impacted every other aspect of my life and the people around me. You may not have a clue what you want right now, that doesn't matter, you just have to know that you know you want something, in whatever area of life that may fall into.

Let's get started, strap in, we are going to be creating your life in a way that excites you. Above all, remember this, an inspired you makes for inspired kids.

Time to announce to the world that you're BACK!

Chapter One

Smashing the "I'm fine syndrome"

"We ourselves feel that what we are doing is just a drop in the ocean. But the ocean would be less because of that missing drop."
Mother Theresa

"COME ON!"

"Why aren't you dressed?"

I look in dismay at the neatly laid out piles of school uniform still sitting there.

"Why do I bother?" I mutter to myself.

To be fair, my eldest, Zak has made a token effort but how has he managed to put his trousers on the wrong way round AGAIN?

"Lita! Lita, sweetheart, come on, please get dressed when you wake up, no, don't give me those big brown sleepy eyes, I know you can do it by yourself."

"TEETH! Have you cleaned your teeth? Zak, stop wondering aimlessly around the place, shoes on NOW! Come on guys, it's the same routine every morning, move it!"

As I look around me, I am amazed, as I am every morning, quite how two small people and one large one (that is my husband) can comprehensively turn our house into a bombsite in the space of an hour. It was immaculate when I flopped into bed last night.

We finally bundle out of the door; amidst wails of dismay as the realisation strikes that they have forgotten some random piece of plastic they promised a friend or something for 'show and tell.'

Meanwhile, I am mentally ticking off book bags, swimming bags, dance gear, football kit, and hoping against hope that I have remembered to sign whatever needed signing for whatever inevitable letter that came home the night before. It's a futile task. I am pretty much guaranteed to have forgotten something. I swear to god that they take more to school in a day than we take travelling for a couple of months.

We arrive, just in time, kids struggling to keep up with a mum on a mission determined not to let team H-K down.

Then with a cuddle and a kiss (although sadly Zak isn't so keen on that anymore) they are gone.

I breathe.

Job done.

Mission accomplished.

As I glance around me, I smile at the familiar, friendly faces of the other Mums, some looking immaculate and serene whilst others fall into the slightly less immaculate and less serene camp.

I ask the inevitable question.

"Hey, how are you are doing?"

"I'm fine, thanks."

Or perhaps:

"Yeah, not so bad."

I'm fine. I'm fine.

Question. How many times a day is that your automatic response?

OF COURSE YOU ARE **FINE!**

You have to be FINE. You're a mother for goodness sake. If you're not fine then everything will fall apart!

As I looked deeper into the eyes of my peers when I ask the question, I know that that is about as far as it goes for some. Fine.

My question to you is… "Is 'fine' good enough for you?"

Really, what does 'fine' mean? It generally means that everything is ok, that life is ticking on, that you are managing to keep on going, doing what you are supposed to be doing. Ticking the boxes.

My friend Katie, however, likes to describe it in a different kind of way (she is Australian; they tell it how it is). She reckons 'fine' is another way of saying f****d up, insecure, neurotic and emotional.

Personally I think that is a little harsh, but as she willingly admits, that was her once and who am I to argue.

But hang on a minute. Is it right to question whether that is enough? I mean really, you are probably not in a position to grumble when you think about how your life compares to most people in the world. Your kids are getting an education, you have a roof over your head and no doubt you manage a holiday or two a year. If you are married or have a partner who is working to support your family then really, you are one of the lucky ones.

When I began to question this, I felt guilty. Why couldn't I be one of those mothers where being a mother was enough? What was wrong with me? Why was I not happy with my lot?

However, if you are anything like me, it isn't enough. It may well be that you have never admitted to yourself that it isn't enough because, quite frankly, that would be incredibly ungrateful.

Well, I am here to tell you that yes, absolutely, you should be grateful. Being grateful is one of the most powerful feelings in the world and should be practiced daily.

But lurking underneath all that, it is quite likely that there is something else going on.

As we are talking woman to woman here, I hope you don't mind but I am going to take a stab at, potentially, what may really be going on if you dare to let yourself really think.

Somewhere hiding beneath the day-to-day domestic whirlwind, you know well that you are a smart, educated, woman who, pre-kids, made your mark in the world. Maybe you were a career woman, maybe you weren't, but what I know is that if you were attracted to this book, you had it going on.

I am not discounting anything that you are doing right now, not at all. I have full respect because I know it is damn hard at times.

I also know that something inside of you is whispering 'there must be more to life than this. I know I can be more, I know I can have more, I know I have more to offer the world.'

You may not have listened to this voice yet, because, well, they are pretty confronting thoughts to be having. Having said that, my overriding purpose for writing this book is to get you to become aware and acknowledge that voice.

Why? Because I know the magic that can happen, when you surrender to it.

A word of warning though, before that magic can happen; you may have to experience something that I can only describe as 'The Wobble'.

The Wobble

'The Wobble' is a point that I would call a defining moment in your life. For some it can be dramatic, for others traumatic. For me it can only be described as slightly ridiculous.

My family and I were away at the time, in Western Australia. It couldn't have been more idyllic; we had hit the road with a beast of an off-road car, a tent and had headed into the sunset. It was pure fun, family time.

Yet something wasn't right and I couldn't put my finger on it.

I was starting to get fed up with my husband constantly fishing, because as the kids were small at the time it was always down to me to look after them. I know, it sounds lovely, I shouldn't grumble. But let me tell you, toddlers on the beach, equals zero relaxation time.

Back at the campsite that night, once the kids were in bed, I was clearly smouldering.

So Babs (my husband) asked, "Come on then Jen, what's wrong with you?"

"Nothing" I grumpily replied.

"Oh come on, don't be ridiculous, of course there is. You are in a strop because I went fishing again."

I proceeded to mumble back something to do with the fact that it was ok for him to do exactly what he wanted all the time, which is highly unfair as he is extremely hands on.

He then said something that led to perhaps not my finest, but certainly my defining moment.

"For God's sake Jen, stop being such a bloody martyr and choose to do something."

How dare he say that! I promptly picked up the fish he had caught and flung it squarely at his head. Nice one Jen.

A rather spectacular strop followed. I stumbled my way down to the beach in the dark and sat stunned at what had happened. Babs and I never argue, so this was quite something. As I sat listening to the waves, feeling like a complete drama queen, I had an overriding outpouring of emotion. The tears came and I couldn't stop them.

I am generally an emotionally stable person, I'm telling you, and this was not normal behaviour! I felt like I was having some kind of Bridget Jones moment but I still couldn't work out what on earth about.

Eventually I went back, to find Babs tucked up in bed with the kids and I couldn't believe that he hadn't come out to try and find me! I snuck in and sobbed silently until finally it hit me. He was absolutely right. I was not choosing to do something with my life.

Oh I was being a good mum, I think, and a good wife, I was even working at the time but it didn't excite me. I was not inspired. I wasn't excited by 'what was next'. I was, once I dared to admit it, deeply unsatisfied with myself. On the surface I had it all, underneath I felt like I was flailing and becoming less and less of the person I knew I could be.

Having kids is such a major milestone in life and as we know, it is all consuming. Everything can take a bit of a nosedive, from your sleep patterns, your confidence and self-esteem, down to your boobs and your pelvic floor. If you were used to a dynamic lifestyle beforehand the repetitive daily patterns can be mind numbing.

Unless you are some kind of super woman or outsource your kids, there is no getting away from it; things change. Your priorities change. The career you once had is more than likely compromised due to your time commitments. Your contributions at dinner party conversations seem a little banal and well, your confidence maybe a little on the low side.

Yet at the same time, you have the most adorable, important beings in your life that you couldn't possibly love more than you do.

And so the conflict simmers.

The question is; should you just muddle on through knowing that you are a person with huge potential and let it go, or risk having your own fish moment when it may just be too late? Mine was ridiculous and salvageable, for others the fallout has been much, much worse.

Unchecked dissatisfaction is the cause of so much heartbreak. Loss of confidence, relationship breakdown, affairs, weight gain and even problems with children is a very real outcome of someone that is trying to suppress their dissatisfaction.

I'm not joking, and it's horrible to witness.

But what I am about to say flies in the face of that.

I WANT you to be dissatisfied.

Huh?

Why dissatisfaction is a good thing

Although dissatisfaction can be incredibly destructive, if you understand what it really means, then it can be the most positive emotion in the world.

Most people get confused between satisfaction and happiness; they are in fact very different things.

During my 'fish period', if anyone had asked me if I was happy I would have said a resounding yes. Seriously, I was. I was very happy with my husband, my kids were a joy to me (well most of the time anyway), I had great friends, a gorgeous home and all things considered, a great lifestyle. I was, in a word, blessed.

But I was still dissatisfied. Being happy wasn't enough. Why not? Well I believe that you are only truly fulfilled in life when you are making progress. That's why some people can have all the money in the world, all materials things money can buy, yet still be dissatisfied.

As human beings we have some basic human needs that need to be met. I never truly understood this until I heard Anthony Robbins talk about it, and suddenly everything slotted into place in terms of understanding. It is when you have greater understanding and self-awareness that you can start to make positive changes in your life. Until then, you remain in the sleep walking state.

Let me explain further because they are so relevant if your kids are heading to school age or are in school. These needs explain why you are feeling frustrated and my goodness, I wish I had had this understanding when I went through this rather than swinging between guilt, fear and neuroticism (hmm, maybe Katie's definition of FINE is spot on after all).

Need 1: Growth

"Unless you try and do something beyond what you have already mastered you will never grow"
Ronald E Osborn

One of those needs is to grow. If you are frustrated right now, I can pretty much guarantee that will be one of the underlying causes, particularly when you are going through the cycle of motherhood.

When you first become a mother, you are stretched to the limit. Everything is completely new, you are on the sharpest learning curve of your life, as let's face it you don't learn how to be a mother before the event. You are well and truly thrown in at the deep end.

In time you get the hang of it, you get into some kind of routine, and in my case it wasn't long before I popped another one out. Up to your eyeballs in nappies, potty training and mush, you don't have time to consider whether or not you are growing, hell, it's all about survival.

Then, all of a sudden, nursery and school are looming, and your thoughts turn to what next. You have reached a new milestone in your life and your spirit is crying out to GROW!

The fact is, whether you are spiritual in your thinking or not, we are a spiritual being in a body suit. Spirit is always looking to expand and be fully expressed.

And that, my friend, is one of the primary reasons you may be out of sync right now. You need to be growing to live a fulfilled life. Dissatisfaction is simply a signal to you that it is time to grow. That is why no matter how much people may have, or how much they have achieved, it is never enough. Their spirit will always be looking to expand and express itself further.

So don't feel guilty about any frustration you are experiencing, don't think that there is something wrong with you if you are not truly satisfied with your lot right now, because you are not meant to be satisfied.

In fact, if you think you are satisfied right now, I am prepared to stick my neck out and say that you are merely sleep walking through life.

The truth is, most people are doing just that. To admit to dissatisfaction forces you into change and most people avoid change like the plague. They would rather stick pins in their eyes. It explains why people stay in abusive relationships, jobs they hate, and live in places that depress them.

If that is you, then that's ok, but perhaps the rest of this book isn't for you. My challenge to you throughout this book is to wake up to your dissatisfaction and you have to be pretty ballsy to do that. But when you do, and embrace it, extraordinary things can occur.

Think about it for a second and look around you. Pretty much everything around you has been created out of someone's dissatisfaction. The mac I am writing on now was born out of Steve Job's dissatisfaction with the design and functionality of existing laptops. The chair I am sitting on evolved from caveman's dissatisfaction of sitting on the floor. Every form of transport is the result of people's dissatisfaction. Are you getting the point?

Dissatisfaction is the beginning of a creative process, and ultimately you are a creative being. That is why we have been given the faculty of imagination. Dissatisfaction is your motivator, it is the reason we go ahead and set goals. When we reach our peak of dissatisfaction, and the pain is too great we are finally moved to do something about it.

So why do we do everything in our power to ignore the signals? Why do we try to deny any kind of dissatisfaction?

Well, do you ever recall as a child being told to be satisfied with what you have? Again this comes back to the distinction between gratitude and satisfaction, they are very different concepts, but perhaps that wasn't explained clearly enough as a child, and with that simple misinterpretation, the damage is done.

If you know you are experiencing an element of dissatisfaction then don't suppress it. It's a good thing. It's time to embrace it. It's time to grow.

Need 2: Contribution

The minute you start growing something else happens. Your ability to contribute something of value to the world also grows. Of course, you are contributing anyway by being a mother, but somehow that belief can get lost on us, mainly because of societal conditioning around the value that is being placed on 'just' being a mother. Both you and I know that there is nothing 'just' about it.

That said we are put on this earth to contribute in some significant way. The most powerful way to contribute is when you are on purpose. Simply put, being on purpose means doing the thing that you, as a unique being, are here to do.

We all have a purpose. Sadly, most people never discover what theirs is as they are caught up in playing it safe, fearful of not being able to pay the bills or moving out of their comfort zone.

You have unique talents and abilities that are part of you, and your greatest contribution to this world is to use them. When you are on purpose, you are contributing in the most effective way you can. Sure, you are more than likely constantly contributing in one way or other, whether that is at the school, to friends, to charity or whatever it is for you.

But when you are growing, progressing in a way that really excites you, that is where your greatest contribution will come.

Before I had kids, for five years I helped grow a charity with a friend of mine who had founded the charity. Although I knew I was making a difference and working on something worthy, it still didn't feel like it was my purpose in life. However when I started to work with women to empower them to get out there and live a life that inspired them, watching the results happen felt like my contribution to the world way surpassed the work I did in marketing for the charity as it was much more aligned with what comes naturally to me.

Before I discovered what I loved to do, I can honestly say that it felt like my contribution to the world was pretty limited. When I had kids I felt reliant on my husband to bring in the money to support us, which is perfectly normal and acceptable, hell, we have our hands full! But at the same time, I began to resent the fact that he was out there interacting with the world, making waves, and I wasn't.

Now this is a completely personal thing. I felt like that. It doesn't mean that you have to feel like that. What I am trying to help you with here is to recognize some of the reasons you are frustrated and for you to know that it is completely normal to feel that way. It is simply because some of your basic human needs aren't currently being met.

Need 3: Significance

Significance! How significant are you feeling? Hmm, now that is an interesting one as a mother. This one can kick off all sorts of emotions. You have an inbuilt need to feel special and important in some way. As a mother you are, of course, incredibly important, no doubt about that. But my question is, do you FEEL special? Do you FEEL unique? Do you FEEL important?

One of our gripes is that we often feel at the bottom of the pile. Everyone else comes first, and it leaves very little 'you' time where you feel like you are truly appreciated.

When you are working or playing a role that elicits appreciation, whether that is in the form of being paid or in the form of praise you get, then that need is fulfilled.

It is a rare thing to feel fully appreciated as a mother. Furthermore, if you know that you are working a job purely because it fits around your hours but you know that it isn't really any reflection of what you are truly worth, then your level of feeling significant is going to be pretty low.

This is, of course, totally compounded when your kids start school. Up until this point they are pretty much totally dependent on you. Yes, they may have gone to nursery, but somehow starting school is different. They are moving into the next phase of their little lives and subsequently so do you.

They are going into a world of influence from others that are not you. Teachers and peers play a major role in their development now. The result? Your feeling of significance, a basic human need, drops.

You may have been looking forward to the day when you finally have some freedom, a bit of time to breathe, to start concentrating on some of the things that you want to do. But the question that often hits us at this time is…what is it that I actually want to do? More often than not, that hasn't been worked out yet.

Leaving you feeling…insignificant.

The more insignificant you feel, your confidence and your belief in actually being able to get out there and do something that you consider to be significant in the world diminishes, week by week.

Again, understand that it is completely normal to feel this way. The challenge now and challenges can always be overcome, is to do something positive with your life that is going to up those levels of significance. Don't panic yet if you have no idea what that is, we are going to get to that.

Your time is now

Up until this point, I have been shedding some light on why your life is maybe in a challenging period. Change is afoot and naturally, it can get a little uncomfortable. I know it all sounds very obvious, and you may well be very aware of it, but I know from experience when I was in it, all I could do was feel the frustration and not rationalize it.

I want to highlight why now is an incredible time for you, to get out there and grasp the opportunity that this stage of life brings. We have all been through different stages in our lives, different stories, and different journeys, to get to where we are but in essence; we have a wealth of experience behind us. I am making an assumption that you are in your thirties or forties if you are reading this and your kids are around school age.

Your late teens tend to be a time of blissful naivety, your life is laid out before you and you can conquer the world, should you choose. Alternatively you bugger off around the world as I did, claiming that the 'experience of travel' is way more valuable than a full-blown career straight away. Admittedly, I took this to the extreme and returned home four and a half years later, but hey, I had a damn good time and horizons were expanded in many ways!

It then becomes about making your mark and proving yourself to the world of 'work' that those years of swilling down the 'pound a pint' at the student union or college bar really did prepare you for work and earning a decent wad of cash every month.

And so the search for a life partner begins, the endless weddings that begin to merge into one, clearly scream out to you that you have moved into 'the next phase', whether you fall into the married category or not. I know for my single friends, life changes dramatically for them as well when everyone around them starts getting married off.

Kids follow and it brings us to now, our present reality. Here's the thing though. Do you have any idea how much you actually learnt in those years? You have a wealth of experience behind you. You have overcome challenges in some form or other. You have made it through having a child for goodness sake! You have so much value locked up inside you right now it would blow your mind if you could just see it.

And yet, many of my peer group that I talk to don't see it. I assure you it is true. Everything you have been through up until this point has been for a reason. And that reason has been to get you to this point. Now your future is laid out ahead of you, it is a blank canvas waiting to be created. No matter what you have got going on in your life right now, I stand by what I say. It is a blank canvas ready to be filled with all sorts of incredible possibilities.

Admittedly, if someone had said that to me pre-fish moment, I would have rolled my eyes and my natural cynicism would have kicked in. I know now it's true. I have worked with too many clients who have started clueless, knowing they wanted to do more with their life but no idea what. They have gone on to achieve extraordinary things. You are no different.

The Truth

At the risk of sounding like a life coach guru, you have unlimited potential and are full of endless possibilities. Unfortunately, that way of thinking is shut down pretty early on in life when we are led to believe that we need to conform in one way or another. The result? A lesser version of who you really are.

If you are genuinely ready to find out what you are capable of and start living a more inspired life, you have to be prepared to take a good look at where you currently are.

So grab yourself a glass of wine, and prepare for some self-reflection. You need to take a good look at each area of life and the key is not to wallow in self-judgment and consume the whole bottle! Let go of all the reasons why you are perhaps not where you would like to be in some areas and congratulate yourself where you feel a sense of satisfaction.

You will inevitably find that certain areas of your life are more progressive than others, and that is completely natural. Then rate yourself out of 10. Be brutally honest with yourself and get emotionally involved with the exercise. Remember dissatisfaction is the key to motivation.

No matter who you are, everyone has a weak area, and there is always room for improvement. Don't forget the 'fine syndrome', fine is going to rate pretty low.

And fear not, we will be looking at these in greater detail in Chapter Three, where you get to pick up the pieces.

Health & Fitness:

- How happy are you with the health of your body right now?

- How satisfied are you with your current level of fitness and body image?

Relationships:

- Husband, partner, friends, family, kids, colleagues – how connected are you?

- How open, honest, and self-expressed are you around these people?

Adventure:

You need adventure in your life.

- When was the last time you felt excited, spontaneous or experienced something new?

Career:

- How satisfied are you currently on the work front?

- If you aren't currently working do you wish you were?

- Or if you are, are you inspired by what you do?

- Does it feel like work?

- Does it get you up in the morning?

Finances:

- How satisfied are you with your finances?

- Are you more than comfortable?

- Is it a constant stress?

- How to you feel when you think about money?

Learning & Development

- Are you learning new things?

- Do you feel like you are growing?

Contribution

- How much do you feel you are contributing to others?

Spiritual

- Do you put any time aside in your day to just 'be' and create a spiritual connection? Whether that is meditating, journaling, walking, running, going to church, or whatever works for you.

This kind of thinking often brings up all sorts of emotions and insecurities; you may find yourself to be a snivelling mess on the floor. On the flip side you can also find yourself pleasantly surprised when you start to give yourself credit for some of the things that you do.

This exercise for me was the start of everything. Seeing the truth down on paper made my dissatisfaction real. It was no longer a fleeting thought that I pushed to the back of my mind. It was real and confronting. I found myself in tears when I looked and started to rate myself in my career and finances; this was where my gaping hole lay. To know that I was an intelligent being yet in this area of life I felt like I had totally underachieved given that I knew, deep down, that I was capable of more.

And so my journey began. As I sit writing this I am smiling because quite frankly it is hilarious to think that I am writing a book as we speak, whereas not so long ago I was utterly lost as to what I wanted to do with my life. I was fearful of the time slipping away, living a mediocre life, and not being an inspiration to my kids. How things change if you allow it.

So embrace this journey, you have no idea where it is going to take you. I for one am excited for you!

Chapter Two

Cracking the confusion

"Nobody can go back and start a new beginning but anyone can start today and make a new ending"
Maria Robinson

You may or may not have taken action on the last chapter. Quite feasibly, as you are a busy woman, you read on through, got some insights and here you are onto the next chapter.

Whether or not you did is purely your choice, and whether you realized it or not, you made a decision to either keep turning the pages or stop and reflect on where you currently are in each of the areas of life.

If you did, then you will have started a process that may well lead to change. If you didn't, then I would say the chances are the rest of this book will remain simply a collection of knowledge that is taken no further.

That's the funny thing about life. Everything you do has a choice attached to it, but the majority of the time you are completely unaware of that. There are so many things we do in our day-to-day life that happen on autopilot. It would be staggering to have to think about how to get out of bed in the morning, how to take every step, how to put on your clothes. But at some point you couldn't do these simple acts. You learnt them and having practiced them over and over again; they have been programmed into you.

So what if the same was true for the way you run your life? What if your life was a series of habits? Unless you are one courageous mama, and are constantly operating outside your comfort zone, then I would declare that that is exactly the case.

The question therefore is, if you could choose to live your life in any way, if you could choose to live wherever you wanted, if you could choose what you did on a daily basis would it be exactly as it is?

The answer to that question is a resounding yes.

Huh?

Yep. You have, in fact, chosen it to be as it is. Your life as it is now is the result of thousands of decisions, most of which are completely habitual, that you have made over the period of your life. If that is true, then that can only mean one thing.

You are wholly responsible for it.

Oooh. That can be a hard one to swallow for some.

That was precisely the reason I felt so shattered that night in Australia. For the first time, probably ever, I realized I had to start taking responsibility for where I was and how I was feeling. Despite my husband being the one that had the fish thrown at his head, I was the one that felt like I had been slapped round the chops with a damp squid.

All was not well with me and I expected a bit of consoling and so life would continue. Not so. Thank the lord, because had that been the case I would more than likely be doing a job that didn't inspire me, wandering on through life thinking that everything was 'fine' whilst having the occasional meltdown.

Instead, in the last couple of years I have learnt, stretched and grown so much that at times I hardly recognize myself. Not only that, the actions that I have taken impacted pretty much everyone around me. I often look around me in awe at how one ripple can impact so many people.

I remember reading once that every thought you have and every action you take, has a ripple effect and changes the landscape of the world forever. I never really understood that, I mean how can one person alone in their personal thoughts really bear any significance on the world unless you were heard loud and clear in the press or communicated with the world in some way.

Yet I have witnessed it to be true. Deciding that night to take responsibility for who I wanted to be and what I wanted to achieve has caused a ripple across the world.

I started by arriving back in the UK and going on a mission to set a whole bunch of goals for myself. I was a girl possessed! Even before my actions and achievements started to become visible to the world, the vibe that I was giving out started to have an impact on those close to me.

"I want a bit of what you're on!" a few people said to me. With encouragement, they went on their way and started to make a few changes in their own life, and so it continued.

In a nutshell because I made a conscious decision to 'wake up' from my slumber, I unintentionally, at the time, disturbed a few others from their snooze.

What if you have had some crazy stuff happen in your life that you are in no way responsible for?

Shit happens. It really does. Inexplicable events, illnesses, and tragedies surround many people in this world and it is a bit far-fetched, in my opinion, to claim that we are responsible for everything, you certainly don't control most things. There is a school of thought that would argue that we attract everything in our lives, but I am left baffled as to how to explain away events such as horrific accidents and natural disasters that destroy people's lives in one fell swoop.

However, as hard as it can be to hear sometimes, I firmly believe you are always faced with a choice as to how you react or respond to a situation and again, your choices would define your life going forward.

Why is it that some people, despite appalling circumstances, shine through with a smile on their face and go on to achieve remarkable things? What is the difference between people who seemingly come from exactly the same environment with the same resources yet can be leading completely different lifestyles? Why is it that some people seem to be permanently 'lucky' and others not?

Well it comes down to one thing.

And it's really very simple.

The decision or choice you make at any given period in time.

So if you want to improve the way things are in your life, you have to learn to make better choices. Sounds easy hey, but why in reality is it not so easy? Why are we so quick to blame other people, conditions and circumstances for the way things are?

Well, my view is that it comes down to two things. Self-awareness and, of course, the way we have been programmed over time which is what ultimately drives us.

Let's look at this in a little more detail.

At any given time, you have the ability to consciously reject or accept any thought that comes into your mind. You also have the ability to consciously choose to react or respond to any given circumstance. It's what makes us human.

But to access this really simple yet powerful tool to start making any kind of change, you have to be aware of it. That requires thinking for yourself!

You might argue at this point that you do think for yourself, you are constantly thinking for yourself, and let's face it as a mother you tend to do the thinking for the rest of your family as well which can be utterly exhausting at times.

As George Bernhard Shaw so aptly says:

> *"Two percent of the people think; three percent of the people think they think; and ninety-five percent of the people would rather die than think."*

Ask yourself, do you really think or do you react? It is perfectly normal to react so don't beat yourself up; it is what we are conditioned to do.

Until I got my head around this, I didn't realize the extent to which I did this. Many of my wants and desires in the past have been rejected immediately due to the ingrained beliefs about the old classics, time and money. Nothing unusual, most people out there hold some kind of limiting beliefs around one or both of them. But now that I am aware of it, I cringe when I think about some of the opportunities that I missed in the past.

Had I stuck to this way of thinking, my last six years would have looked very different! As you read the following example think back over time of some of the decisions you have made, and on what basis have you made them.

Six years ago, my husband's brother and family moved over to Western Australia. There was initial excitement about how we would visit them, but when it came down to it I put my foot down. My husband was pushing to go yet all I could see was the state of our circumstances at the time. In my mind, there was no way on earth that we could afford the time and more importantly the money. Zak was very young, my husband's marketing agency had folded and he was just starting out on a new business. There was nothing in our reality at the time that said it was possible.

My husband however, is persistent to say the least. His response was:

"We're going for a couple of months. It's important. We'll work it out."

At which point I would launch into him with every single reason why we couldn't. I fought with all my energy against the very thing I wanted most in the world.

Was I thinking for myself? No! Did I choose to accept the thought that we could go? No. I made the decision that it wasn't possible based on our current circumstances, based on the fact that nobody else around us was swanning off for a couple of months, that we didn't have a stable income and on and on I went.

Well, he won. I had to ask for the time off from work, which to my amazement was granted even though I had had time off for maternity, and we went. Lesson learnt; if you don't ask you will never know the answer.

Did the world collapse around us? Err, no, far from it, it was amazing. The time we got to spend together as a family was priceless. We worked from there when we could, everything remained intact and little by little I began to change.

The next year came around and my husband proposed we went again. Bang. Straight away I went into panic mode. I was pregnant with Lita, still, we were financially unstable and so I fought my corner once again, although perhaps this time with not so much gusto.

We are now in year seven and I have just booked our tickets again. It has become, dare I say it, a habit. I don't give it a second thought. It is part of what we do as a family, and everything else is worked out around it. The kids have a fantastic relationship with their Australian cousins, and have experienced more in their little lifetimes than I did in the first 18 years of my life. They are growing up with an understanding that work can be built around the lifestyle you want. I very much doubt that they will have a future where they feel constrained by what they can and can't do.

School has started and yet we still go and incorporate an element of home-schooling while we are there. There will come a time in the next year or so when we will question whether we continue but that is simply another decision based on what we feel is right at the time. Many people write off decisions like that because they believe they are constrained by the school system. It's not so. They are your children, you decide. Many kids around the world are successfully home-schooled as families set off to travel together. It's possible, it's your decision, and it's dependent on your values, not 'the system'.

I am not saying any of this to brag about what a wonderful life we have. I am trying to make the point that everything comes down to the choices you make in life. I remember last year a friend of mine asking when we were heading off this year. I told him in a couple of weeks and he literally slumped in front of me.

"God I wish I could do that" he said. "You have no idea how lucky you are."

Not lucky. We've just chosen to see life in a different way. For my husband it was more natural, I, however, had to learn it. There are people who say, well it's okay for you, you have family out there. But that's not the point. It's not about whether or not you can go to Australia or wherever it is that you would like to go. It's about whether or not you recognize opportunities when they come your way and what you do with them.

I still get caught up in my limiting beliefs around time and money, but my level of awareness of it is so much more heightened that I am able to step back and consider before I write anything off.

Most people wouldn't recognize an opportunity if it came up to them and smacked them round the chops because their conditioning is so strong that everything is immediately rejected and shut down.

The whole purpose of this chapter is to start to open your eyes, raise your awareness, to get into the habit of just stopping before you make an automatic decision on things. You may still make the same decisions but at least you would have thought about it.

To not make a decision is to make a decision

It's funny, many people I know will openly admit that they are no good at making decisions and they spend their days in torment, or worse still allow everyone else, be it friends, family or even the state of the economy, to make those decisions for them.

What they don't realize however is that to not make a decision is to make a decision. The minute you let external circumstances make decisions for you, your path has been chosen.

These decisions can be of seemingly large or small impact, but the fact is, all of them contribute to the point of how fulfilled you are right now in your life.

Let's take a different example, one that wasn't so life changing, yet all the same created a different outcome to what would have happened if I hadn't been aware that I could choose as to whether I reacted or responded to the situation.

My husband and I had flown to Denmark for a wedding. It was a real treat as it was one of the first times we had been away together without the kids. On the morning of the wedding we were running a little late (now that is a habit that we have to DECIDE to break!) and as he was ironing his shirt, I asked if he would iron my dress.

The next thing I heard was him swearing profusely and I looked up to see that he had turned a pale shade of white which is no mean feat as he is half Indian. I followed his eyes down to see a brown stain in the middle of my cream dress.

The world stopped for a minute. I opened my mouth to yell at him, yet somewhere, in the back of my mind was a little voice saying: "React or respond Jen, react or respond."

Very calmly, I breathed, smiled and said, "Don't worry babe, it was an accident, I'm sure I can wear something else."

At which point his jaw dropped to the floor. The moment was gone, I stayed in a good mood and we spent the day together having a lot of fun. How different could that have been? Had I chosen to react, my mood would have affected him, he would have felt guilty all day and the snatched opportunity to spend time together without the kids would have been ruined.

Hardly life changing I know. However, these things add up and determine how loving your relationships are with everyone you are close to. Your reactions shape how your kids grow up. They are like sponges; they learn from you and take it into their future.

Having said that, nobody is perfect. I still frequently lose the plot with the kids when I allow them to push the right buttons. But I try more and more to think in this way, and if I do react, my ability to apologize quickly has strengthened.

Why is it so hard to make decisions and how do you become more proficient?

Why aren't we all doing exactly what we would love to do in life if all it took was making the decision to do it?

You've never been taught how!

Have you ever really been taught how to make decisions? Given that it is one of the most useful skills to have and that our proficiency at it shapes our entire life you would think it would be at the top of the educational agenda. Sadly though, it certainly wasn't when I was at school. In fact it was more along the lines of rote learning and follow the path of conformity. Thankfully, I am witnessing a little more forward education with my kids at school but it is worth bearing this in mind with your own kids to have it as an exercise to have them practice often!

The fear factor

Being afraid of making the wrong decision about something has to be right up there for most people. Again, you may not be aware of it but more often than not that is what is holding you back. Endless scenarios are played out in the mind and whether it is the fear of failing, the fear of success or the fear of making a complete fool of yourself, they all creep in there, clouding our abilities to make decisions.

We are so afraid of getting it wrong! The 'what ifs' drive our thinking, leaving no decisions made and so the frustration deepens.

Let me tell you the truth. If you are trying to decide whether to play a bigger game in life, and this is something I have really discovered the last couple of years since I decided to step it up, you're going to fail whether you make the decision or not.

Ouch. Well that wasn't very motivational, was it? However, it is absolutely true.

If you are reading this book, something tells me that there is a part of you reaching out to grow as discussed in the last Chapter. Your spirit is willing you to step on out and take on something new in the world. If you decide not to, then you will remain 'fine' (and we all know what that means now), life will continue but I can guarantee you that your dissatisfaction and the feeling of being unfulfilled will grow.

On the other hand, if you do make a decision to step out of your comfort zone and take a leap of faith on anything that is worthy of you, well, the chances are there are going to be some stumbling blocks on the way. I am yet to find anyone who is aiming high that makes a success of things over night. Take the infamous story of Thomas Edison and the number of times it took him to create the first lasting light bulb. It took around 10,000 tries.

A reporter asked Edison. "How many times are you going to fail at creating the light bulb?"

Mr Edison replied, "I haven't failed! I have simply discovered another way not to invent the light bulb."

Do you seriously think that if you are facing a big decision, that challenges attached to that decision won't follow? Of course, they will. Don't decide not to do something just in case it doesn't work out. Understand that adjustments will probably be needed along the way until you achieve your desired goal. See failure as feedback, feedback that an adjustment is needed. Embrace this mindset and your ability to make decisions will skyrocket.

You have no idea where you're heading

This is similar to values. No vision, no map, and no idea what an inspired life looks like for you. The fastest way to let life pass you by is to have no vision. You end up wandering aimlessly through life from one day to the next, with no real purpose other than getting through the day.

Without a vision or specific goals that you are working towards you are going to be operating full steam ahead on autopilot. And, as discussed previously, when you are on autopilot you will let outside conditions and circumstances determine your fate, rather than you choosing.

I must admit when I first had babies I was totally in this space (understandably, I say). Getting through a day was momentous, getting through a night was nothing short of a miracle. But times change, and as you find your groove with your kids you begin to have more of a capacity for other things in your life. Unfortunately, what can happen, as it did for me, is that time suddenly comes and you're not prepared for it. Rather than sitting down and creating this awesome vision for yourself to set you on a path, you go into panic and frustration mode, the end result for many being a drop in self-esteem and confidence.

Significant change will only ever occur if the pain is too great for things to stay as they are, or you are inspired enough to take action. If you're just 'fine' with no vision, then expect more of the same with confusion reigning when it comes to making decisions.

You don't know the 'how'

How many times have you decided not to do something because you didn't know how you were going to do it? It could be a holiday that you would love to take, a new career move or a business you would love to set up; goodness knows how many unborn ideas there are in you. You've thought about it, then dismissed it immediately because you simply haven't got a clue how to achieve it.

Big mistake. Countless opportunities wasted.

That said, this is a pretty tough concept to get your head around. Make a decision without knowing the how. According to the experts, the 'how' will show up.

Is this true? I was pretty sceptical when I first tried to get my head around this concept, but the more I began to implement it into my life, plus seeing the results of clients who embraced the concept then I would say, yes. It truly is quite remarkable. But it only works for you if there's an extra element in place.

It has to be a committed decision.

There is a huge difference between a flaky decision and a committed one. A committed decision is one where you put your neck on the line and actually commit to something.

I did this when I figured out what I wanted to do. I had to invest a pretty hefty sum into my training and I didn't have it. But with this in mind, I signed up and figured I would work it out. I had no idea where it was going to come from, I hadn't spoken to anyone else about it but I made that one mental move that has completely reshaped my future.

I was lucky and the resources showed up.

When you make a shift in your thinking, you begin to attract into your life the people, resources and circumstances that are in harmony with your new focus, thinking and actions.

If you set yourself a big enough goal, you are never going to know the 'how' for all the steps to achieving it. But that shouldn't stop you making a decision to do something. You have to create an element of faith that will see you put one foot in front of the other and take one action at a time. The next step will be revealed as you progress.

I will never forget the first time my husband took me to an isolated piece of land in Morocco in the High Atlas Mountains, south of Marrakech. There before me lay this beautiful plateau with absolutely nothing there. No water, no electricity, no community. He and his brother made the decision to buy it, with the future aim of building villas on it. You need to understand here that neither of them had any property development experience, no knowledge of Morocco and yet, on the back of a loan they bought it.

I am fairly used to him having big ideas but this one I really struggled to get my head around! However, somewhere, in their heads laid a vision that only they could see.

They took one action step, which was to get an 80-year-old Moroccan guy up to the land with two sticks. He was a water diviner, and after much convulsing on certain areas of the land he gave them a toothless grin and confirmed the presence of water.

And so it all began.

Believe me; he had no idea how he was going to achieve the vision. But the first crucial step had been taken, a committed decision, regardless of knowing the how.

Step by step the vision is unfolding, and as I write this I have just got back from a trip out there. It is one of the most incredible developments I have ever seen. The team, the clients, the resources, the builders, the design, the planning all showed up.

Not without sweat and tears might I add, but nonetheless as he persists and continues to take action, this vision that has been in his head for the last five years is taking shape.

Tune into your intuition

Your ability to make decisions is going to be so much harder if you are constantly stuck in your head. Lord knows, I have learnt this.

I went through a period about eight months ago that I just couldn't get clear on anything. I was going round and round in circles trying to work out in what direction I should take my business. It drove me nuts.

Then I realized that I had totally disconnected from the other voice in my head, the voice that comes from your heart and soul. It was as if I had turned my intuitive switch off. No matter how much learning or mentorship I had, I simply couldn't make decisions and so I remained firmly stuck.

Listening to your intuition is key to being able to make decisions to move you forward. We all have this inner guidance system, but whether or not you choose to listen to it is a completely different matter.

How to hone your intuition would require a whole different book but, in short, you need to give yourself the space to do it. Some do it through meditation, others through stream of consciousness writing, and if you're like me then a good solitary walk or run generally does the trick. For this to be effective, it needs to be practiced often to the point where it becomes a habit. Crack this though and your ability to make decisions will become effortless.

So what are you up for?

In this chapter, I have covered the two steps that you need to be able to do before you can start the exciting bit where you get to let your creative juices run wild.

You have to first take responsibility for where you are right now. Be grateful for everything; know that everything to date has been shaping you for this moment when you get to take over as the director of your life. Quit blaming any external circumstances and people who you perhaps believe have made the journey to date a bumpy one. If you have had a smooth ride to date, then yay for you.

Then go ahead and start being much more aware of the choices you are making both on a day-to-day basis and for your future. Check in with yourself regularly to see if you are reacting or responding to situations. Remember, you ALWAYS have a choice. Get good at responding and you will find your days lighter, brighter and a lot more fun!

Chapter Three

What do you want?

"You were given life; it is your duty (and also your entitlement as a human being) to find something beautiful within life, no matter how slight"
Elizabeth Gilbert, Author of Eat, Pray, Love

The question is, are you ready? Are you really ready to acknowledge what is going on for you and make a decision to make some changes? Making a decision is the crucial starting point but you are going to have to work hard on yourself if you are genuinely looking to make a lasting change, which will be challenging.

The question you have to ask yourself next is, is it worth it? Or, if things really are 'fine' right now, is it not better to leave things be? The answer is a resounding yes it is worth it! This is your life we are talking about here; you have one shot at it. If you are feeling dissatisfied it is the spiritual side of you (the bit that really knows) giving you a clear message that you are ready to grow. There is so much more for you to experience. I always think it is a good wakeup call is to imagine yourself at your own funeral. Ok, a bit depressing I know, but what would people be saying about you? What do you want to be remembered for? What legacy do you want to leave your family or this world?

You are already an incredible person; we all are in our own way. You have already achieved remarkable things in your life (you've given birth for goodness sake). If you are not aware of that then you are too busy comparing yourself to other people. This is crucial for you to understand in order to recognize the potential that you have in you for this next stage of life.

The truth is, you can be, do and have anything you want. You have power locked up inside of you that if you truly understood its magnitude you would be walking around with your jaw on the floor.

There are two main reasons why people never get even close to fulfilling their potential. Firstly, they simply don't recognise it in themselves and secondly they don't know what they want.

Let's look at both of these in a bit more detail.

You: The Power House

Here's the bottom line. Everything you need to achieve what you desire to become, or have in life, is already here ready and waiting for you.

I have already mentioned in Chapter 1 that anything that has ever been invented has been created out of someone's dissatisfaction. Initially it is created in the imagination, then, with a strong will, desire and above all, persistence, the desire moves into form in the physical reality.

The Wright Brothers, who invented the first flying machine, were hardly the first people to think about flying. But they wanted it badly enough, and slowly but surely after a great deal of failures they pieced together everything they needed to make it happen. Was everything they needed already there? Absolutely! It just took applying the one powerful tool we all have. That tool is your mind.

Maxwell Maltz states in no uncertain terms quite how powerful this is in his book Psycho Cybernetics:

"The brain is roughly three pounds, yet it contains the equivalent of entire cities full of giant buildings full of computer circuitry."
Maxwell Maltz

If you can grasp the basics of how your mind works you will begin to understand that it has the power to give you anything you want. On the flip side, it can also have the power to destroy everything if it isn't understood or managed in the right way.

At any point in time you are surrounded by an infinite supply of power. Based on people's belief systems it is either referred to as God, energy or the Universe, take your pick.

Your mind has the capability of taking this energy and turning it into thoughts and ideas and, by using your imagination you can create an image in your mind of anything you desire, whether that is a new house, a new business, a toned body, whatever it is that you want.

If you get emotionally involved enough in an idea that you formed with your imagination, then your body will literally be moved to take an action step in some form towards bringing that idea into its physical form. When you start to act a different way, you start to attract the people, circumstances and resources that are now in harmony with your new reality. This is widely known as the Law of Attraction. Please note here that the key to this is the action you take, it isn't simply a case of thinking positively as some people like to think!

So if there is forever an infinite supply of energy ready and waiting for you to turn it into some form, does it not stand to reason that the only thing that limits the amount of power that is used is your own imagination and desire?

Well, in theory yes, but in practice we choose to limit the wattage of power we use by allowing other people, our fears and lack of self-belief to dictate what we think we are worthy of and therefore the images you create in your mind. As quoted by James Allen in his widely influential book, As a Man Thinketh:

"You will become as small as your controlling desire; as great as your dominant aspiration"
James Allen

If you want to understand the degree to which you personally have tapped into this power, then simply look at your life and the results you have had in your life to date, as this is a map of the way you have been thinking!

As we move on in this chapter I want you to now acknowledge that all those fears and lack of belief are real, and then simply park them just for now (well permanently would be good but highly unrealistic I know), as I will be focusing on these in subsequent chapters.

Knowing what YOU really want

Now that you technically know that you have unlimited potential and you know that you have a choice as to whether or not you choose to tap into it, let's move onto the second reason why people aren't fulfilled in life. Quite simply it comes down to not knowing what they really want. If you don't know what you truly want then you are going to struggle to make decisions that will serve you in leading an inspiring and fulfilled life.

From an early age we have learnt to go through life gathering information and searching for answers from external sources, whether that is studying at school or college, books, parents, friends and the media. More often than not, the decisions you make in life, whether you are aware of it or not, are based around what other people are thinking or doing.

Although there is nothing wrong with looking to other people for inspiration, there is a danger in thinking that you want to be 'just like' them. It's totally unrealistic as you can only ever be 'just like' you.

I used to be envious of people I met that radiated energy. They loved their life, they loved what they did and they seemed to be able to get an immense amount done in a short period of time. From time to time they would come up against challenges yet they always seemed to be able to focus purely on discovering the solution rather than dwelling on the problem.

For a while there, I believed they had something that I didn't. Why didn't I have the drive, motivation and energy that they had? How did they discover what made them tick when I was struggling so hard to do so? It wasn't just in the work and business environment. I would meet Mums who were genuinely fulfilled by dedicating their life to their kids. I would compare myself to them and end up feeling guilty and question myself, did the fact that it wasn't enough for me make me a bad mother?

The answer to that was, of course, no. It was right for them, but not for me. I have since come to understand that fulfilment is a deeply personal thing. It's also not something that you 'have' one day; you can't get it. You can only 'be' it. And in order to become something you have to go inside and quit the external search.

The key to unlocking the answer to the question of 'what do I really want to be, have and do' lies in knowing exactly who you are, what you are about, what you stand for and what motivates you. This is otherwise known as you knowing your core values. When you consciously start to live your life according to these, decision-making becomes easy and it is virtually impossible not be living on purpose and have an inspired life.

Every single successful person you meet, and by success, I mean living a fulfilled life; will be consciously aware of the above. They know what their highest values are (i.e. what is most important to them) and they align their entire life to them. Their vision and goals for different areas of life are aligned to their values and as a result, they remain inspired and motivated to achieve, regardless of what obstacles may come their way.

On the other hand, when you are out of sync and misaligned with your highest values, you become frustrated, uninspired, easily distracted and that sense of purpose slowly diminishes.

Understanding the significance of your values changing over time

Before we look at how to identify your highest values it is important to recognize that your value set and their hierarchy will change over time.

If you regularly check in with yourself to identify the hierarchy of your values, you will continually be inspired from within, as to how to move forward in life in a way that is on purpose for you.

At different periods in your life, different values are going to be important to you. During any given period you should be focusing your energy and activity on what you perceive to be important that is missing or you want 'more' of. As you fulfill a value, then others will appear causing perpetual growth.

There are natural transitions in life, which results for most people, in natural shifts in values. Having a child is probably the most obvious of those transitional periods. Pre child or children, you may have held your social life as your highest value and suddenly your family values shift above your social life. You naturally want to spend more time at home with your baby and your actions will reflect that. When your child is approaching school age or starts school it is another classic time for values to be shifting as time opens up for you.

Unease can often creep in during this process when a void that needs filling appears in your life, as deep down you know change is required to fill it.

This is exactly what happened to me. When I went through the exercise outlined in Chapter 1, where I rated where I was at in each area of the seven areas in my life, I discovered some gaping holes that I had been ignoring. In some areas of my life at the time such as spiritual connectivity were rated low, (oh how things change with understanding) and actually that was fine with me, I had no great motivation at the time to do anything about that. It was of low value to me. But when I came to assess my career success and learning and development my chest tightened and an element of panic set in.

You can physically feel where the voids exist that really matter to you. When you can physically feel something in your body, it is your subconscious mind, which is the emotional part of your mind, giving you an inspired message from deep inside you. In my case, it was telling me that the time had come to put all my energy into discovering a new career path in life and to do that I felt the need to educate myself. After a week or so of resistance which was all fear based with old favourites such as I don't have enough time or I don't know enough about anything, I resolved to myself that I would discover what I was supposed to do in life.

Before I went through this evaluation process I hadn't even pinpointed where the heart of my frustration lay. I just knew that it felt like something was missing. In the past (and certainly since having kids) my career had never been high on my list of values. I was working with my husband on his property development business. It was convenient. It fitted around my highest values at the time, which were my kids, and the freedom of time (my 'boss' was very understanding about me working my hours around the kids) and I didn't have a yearning to change anything. But clearly, when the frustration started to creep in it was an indication that my values had changed.

Once I allowed myself to feel what the problem was, I identified that I was inspired to create a business that I loved and I could call my own rather than supporting other people's visions as I had always done in the past. At this stage I had no idea what that would look like, but making the decision to do this in some form or other was enough to get me on the journey to discovering what that might look like.

Your values are an inbuilt automatic correction system

To be fulfilled is a continually adjusting process and unless you know your own values and their order of importance at any one time, you are in danger of getting off track.

Three months after getting my business up and running, I found myself in a situation again where I felt uneasy and dissatisfied. I had successfully launched myself into my training and subsequent coaching business and had more clients than I could handle, but the way I was running the business was out of sync to my other highest values which for me were my family, my freedom around time and freedom of geography (it is very important to me to be able to work from anywhere in the world).

The reality was, that day in and day out, I had groups of people that I was coaching coming into my home at set hours, day and night and my husband was forced to eat meals in the bedroom! Given that one of my highest values is to be able to support my family, that clearly wasn't working. Also, the minute we took off to Australia the business dried up, as I was physically required to be at home, face to face with clients.

Looking back I can see that my subconscious mind had taken over, forcing me back to live by my highest values. I effectively 'sabotaged' the business in the form that I had it. At this point, had my business not been high on my value system I would probably have given up and taken the decision that it wasn't going to work out.

But, as it was still right up there for me, I was inspired from within to find a way to continue with my business as it was still high on my value list, but now I knew I needed to discover how to do it in a way that it served my other high values. This took me on a steep learning curve on how to grow a business online with the ultimate goal of being able to work with people anywhere in the world wherever I happen to be.

During this learning process I met with many challenges, doubts and frustrations. However, because I am so inspired by my vision that I have now consciously built around my core values, I am prepared to learn and do whatever it takes, whether that is investing in myself, or public speaking. For the record, public speaking terrifies the hell out of me. Do I do it? Yes. Is it taking me towards my vision? Yes. Is it getting easier? Yes, in fact I would go as far to say that once I am up there, I enjoy it.

Once you have identified and made a decision to 'fill a void' that is most valuable to you, flashes of inspiration will come to you from the subconscious side of you, guiding the way. Your value system essentially acts as an automatic mechanism to keep you on track towards fulfilling your purpose.

Why most goals fail

The biggest take away from this, or certainly the greatest lesson I have learnt that I want to share with you, is the minute you try to imitate the success of another person you are setting yourself up for failure. True, they may at that very point in time have exactly the same hierarchy of values but given that these change over time, it is unlikely that you will have always been aligned.

There is absolutely no point in creating a vision or setting goals for yourself until you are really clear on what is important to you.

I have identified people in my field of work that I look up to and for a while, there I wanted to be just like them. One person in particular is so incredibly inspiring as a person that I thought I wanted to get to the point that they are at. The reality is that they have been constantly on the road for years perfecting their art, living in hotels and rarely at home with their family for extended periods. It is so far removed from what is really important to me in life that there was no way I was going to succeed in this way.

How do you identify your own values?

The next step then is clearly to identify your own values and make sure you are crystal clear on them before you start to consider the question of what you should be doing to get the inspiration back in your life.

The best way to do this is to start broad and revisit the exercise in Chapter 1 and look at each area of your life and identify what is currently most important to you. Ask yourself the question, what do you really feel you want more of?

For example, if you value your physical exercise and health then you will more than likely have rated yourself highly and it is likely that you are self-motivated to achieve in this area. Taking this a step further, if I asked you to write twenty goals around this particular value, your ideas would probably flow easily from you and you would become inspired by the challenges you set yourself. To those that have this as a low value it would not seem like you were 'missing' something in this area. But to you, if it were a high value, your vision for what is possible would be so much greater, driving you to reach the next level.

Health and fitness happens to rank highly in both my husband and my value system. It is non-negotiable for us and absolutely has to feature in our lives. We recently set ourselves the challenge of a DVD programme called Insanity, which is an intense 60-day programme with one day off a week. We didn't miss one day, and most of the time we completed the forty minutes to an hour session of intense interval training before the school run. People around us thought we were nuts. We rose to the challenge and there was never any doubt that we would complete it. Why? Because at that point in the year it was top on the list on our values! We felt that our fitness was at the time 'missing something', hence the challenge.

On the flipside, if physical exercise and health are relatively low on your value system then the results in your life around this area will tell you that it just isn't important enough for you. You require an immense amount of external motivation to keep you going, that's if you even get going in the first place. Think about those countless New Year's resolutions that are set and broken by week two in January. Why? Because the people that set them simply don't value them enough. The minute it gets challenging or something you value more over exercise and healthy eating comes along, the goal goes out the window.

So, there are going to be some areas of life where you rated yourself poorly, and yet you feel completely indifferent to it. They are simply low on your values and it is not worth focusing your attention on these for now.

Then there are areas that are poorly rated but you feel emotional about the gap, as I highlighted earlier with regard to my career. If you really allow yourself to open up there will be some element that is missing that switches on the emotions. Clients I have worked with, who have genuinely got involved in the process, are often moved to tears when they identify and admit to themselves that something is missing. It's completely natural (hell I was a snivelling mess when I sat there looking at my blank sheet of paper around my career). It's emotional because your subconscious mind, which is the emotional part of your mind, is highlighting what is missing and what is important to you.

The gaps that you identify become your purpose to fill at any given moment in time. In my opinion this takes away the, quite frankly, intimidating task of trying to immediately discover your life's purpose. There are many people out there paralyzed in life because they are searching and searching to discover 'the thing', the one reason they are on this planet, which is traditionally what your purpose is defined as. Sure, there are people out there that are clear on that, and you will be too, but my advice to you is continue to focus on what is important to you in life and find a way to contribute and serve others and you will be well and truly 'on purpose'.

To help you delve deeper into identifying your highest values ask yourself the following questions, as the answers won't lie:

What are you spending your money on?

One of the main giveaways is your bank account. Your bank account will tell you what you value most in the world as you are prepared to part with a valuable resource for something that has more value to you.

If you were to look at my bank account over the past year you would clearly see that money has been spent on family travel, training and education (personal growth and business strategy), and education (including sports) for the children. This year I have spent very little on socialising, clothes and beauty, or material items for our home, they have all been low priorities for me and hence are currently low values for me.

What are you willing to spend time and energy on?

You are motivated to put time and energy into the things in life that you value. Obvious I know, but how often do you take time out to observe this? If I was to suddenly free up three days for you, tell you money was no object and took away all your 'shoulds', what would you choose to do in that time? I think you will find that it is what you value most!

What gets your attention?

When you are flicking through a magazine, the TV, or overhearing conversations, what gets your attention? What do you naturally tune into? This question will help you to drill down into a specific topic or group of people on which to focus your attention.

How would your friends describe you in terms of your strengths and weaknesses?

If you were to ask a close friend and a colleague to describe your strengths and weaknesses, what would they say? It's a good idea to physically do this exercise rather than just guessing based on your perception. Ask them to be completely authentic rather than just pleasing you. The results will either be a surprise or not, but either way it is a great insight into how you are valued by the people around you.

What do people seek advice from you for?

Monitor your conversations with people. What do friends and family value your input in? What do conversations with you often end up being about? When do you find yourself incorporating personal stories into your conversations to demonstrate your experience in an area?

What are you absolutely not willing to negotiate on in life?

This one is key. I also believe that when you reach your thirties or forties you are much, much clearer on this. Answering this question alone, will give you your highest values and their order. Interestingly I have discovered that people are afraid to say these out loud as they perceive that their options will become limited. But surely that is the point? If you want an inspiring life then you have to be able to make a stand for what you believe in and cut out the 99% of things that will not fulfil you!

Take a look at all your answers, look for the emerging patterns and think about what they really mean to you. What is coming up again and again? What do you know in your heart is absolutely 'non-negotiable' for you?

For example, if family travel figured highly on your answers then having a job that had a strict 20 days holiday a year policy would only result in frustration for you and limit you in being able to fulfil that value. You would be demotivated and resentful of your work or business and it would negatively impact your family life.

If, however, travel was important to you but not necessarily with the family, you may be fulfilled in a role that required travelling as part of your job. If that were the case, a business or job role that required you to travel with work would be very fulfilling.

Can you see here why the more specific you are about your values that lie at the heart of you, the more effective the 'map' you will be equipped with to make decisions that serve you towards leading a fulfilled and inspiring life?

None of this is rocket science. You could probably tell me the answers to all of these now. In fact, I know that you know. The question is, are you prepared to live into your values, even if they don't 'fit' the mould of what the people are doing around you or what is expected of you?

I often have the conversation with my now 90 year-old Granny who is constantly trying to understand what I do and how we can possibly live our life the way we do. She often reminds me that in her day they had to bloody well get on with it, whether you liked it or not. Things are different now and we think so very differently to both her and my parents' generation. The opportunities open to us now with the support of technology and the virtual proximity of the rest of the world means that the world truly is our oyster. Whatever we want to be, do, or have is there for the taking (obviously within socially responsible parameters).

Remember, you are doing yourself and those around you that you love, the greatest disservice by not identifying and living to your highest values. You have the ability to create the life you want and it all comes down to the choices you make.

You are now The Creative Director of your life (even if you haven't got a clue what you want to do)

"With every experience, you alone are painting your own canvas, thought by thought, choice by choice"
Oprah Winfrey

Actually, you've always been the Creative Director of your life, but perhaps you haven't been aware of it. The minute you start to do it consciously and with intention, your mojo is going to start coming back (or maybe for the first time) and quite frankly you will be dumbfounded as to the synchronicities that will start occurring for you when you are aligned to what you are 'putting out there'.

You may or may not be looking for the answer to a career move. It really doesn't matter; the process is the same. For you it may be about your relationships, your health, or maybe you are looking for a bit more adventure in your life. It's whatever is most important for you right now. And the wonderful thing about this is, once you start to work on one part of your life, aspirations you have for other areas just seem to start happening. Momentum is the name of the game.

Whatever it is for you, I believe the same holds true. Deep down you know what you want to do, be or have, you just don't allow yourself to even think about it due to the fear and the enormity of saying it out loud. Whether you have allowed yourself to be conscious of it or not is a different matter.

It's your birthright to be excited about life. I love what Kate Winslet has to say on this matter. Love her or hate her you can't dispute the fact that she has grabbed life by the balls and gone for it.

"I wouldn't dream of working on something that didn't make my gut rumble and my heart want to explode!"
Kate Winslet

Read that again and again. Feel it, and imagine what it would be like to feel like that about life.

I will never forget sitting in a group with one of the first clients I ever had, who was also a friend of mine who was up for being a guinea pig. We used to meet in a mastermind group, learning about the principles of success. After a few weeks we moved on to a vision and goal setting programme and when the discussion arose around the question of what it was that you would love to do, the resistance in from this particular girl was immense. She hit an absolute blank.

I had asked them to write down the kind of lifestyle they would like in an ideal world and she simply couldn't write anything down. Nada. Finally, as we worked through the process the following week she very quietly said, with a great deal of emotion that she wanted to be an artist. To admit that to herself was a massive deal. Everything was screaming at her as to why this was ridiculous. How could she possibly make a living doing that? She had a child to bring up; she was a successful event manager in London, which had absolutely nothing to do with being an artist.

But she had uttered that word. What's more, she had uttered that word in the company of others who were rooting for her. Fast forward two years and she now has her own business successfully selling her art. It's been a journey for sure to get her to this point, but the minute she had identified one of her highest values to be creative and committed to herself to live into this, the journey for her began.

You are not suddenly going to come up with 'the thing' that is going to tick all your boxes and inspire you for the rest of your life. It simply isn't realistic. But what you can do right now is start the process and you do that by being honest with yourself by writing down your top five values in order and ask yourself one incredibly empowering question…

If you didn't believe it was impossible, what would you do?

It's that simple. Totally suspend disbelief and allow your imagination to take a free rein, just for now.

Think big to get used to using your imagination again. It doesn't mean you have to take on the world, it means being audacious in your world. You will find absolutely no inspiration in thinking small. Your vision has to drive you forward, inspire you when times are tough, you should have to stretch and grow to achieve it.

Don't try to squash yourself into a box of what is already out there that might suit you. Don't get caught up in desperately trying to work out what you are passionate about because chances are, that one of the reasons you are reading this book is because you can't identify 'your passions'. What's more, there are many people out there that are working in an industry that they are passionate about, yet in a role that bores the pants off them.

Focus on feeling alive first. What would your lifestyle be? Are you a morning person? Would you love to wake up to a run on the beach or would that be your worst nightmare? Do you love to be around people, networking and connecting or do you prefer to work in your own creative space? Do you have the freedom around the kids' school holidays if that is important to you?

Build an image based on feeling alive. We think in pictures and you have to have a clear picture in your mind to enable you to get emotionally involved in the idea enough to recognise opportunities that are aligned to you when they come your way and act on them. They always will have been there, you just haven't been aware of them.

When I started this journey I had absolutely no idea what I wanted to do, I just knew I wanted to do something and I knew that I had to have control around my time, so that I could always be there for the kids and that I could be 100% authentically me.

Bit by bit I realized that I had always had a fantastic lifestyle (subconsciously I have always lived to my core values) and it was something people had often asked me how I managed it. Naturally, I have always loved to inspire others to get out there and do what they loved. Literally, the day after I verbalized that to myself an email dropped from thin air into my inbox about a training programme that would give me the relevant training to put that into practice in a business. The decision was quickly made to do it because I knew by that point what I was about. That's not to say that that is that, job done. It is an evolving process and things change as you change and your understanding depends.

You have to get in the right frame of mind to start. Now is your chance. Write. Imagine. Create. Write every morning before you start your day; let the pen write whatever comes to mind from your subconscious, all the answers lie there.

Here are a few pointers to start your creative juices flowing. As you read the following, know that some areas will be of a lower value than others so don't write anything down just because you think you 'should'. I'll say it one last time and by now you must be sick of reading it, make sure whatever you write is aligned to what is important to you!

Health & Fitness

Love it, hate it, or indifferent. When something happens to your health, it would without question become your most important value in the world. All areas of your life are important, but I guess this one you can't do without, no matter what you want to achieve.

If maintaining a good physique naturally motivates you, then you won't require additional inspiration. But if you're not you have to tap into a good enough reason why to get off your butt and do something about it. It's not about looking good; it's about enabling you to do all those other things in life that you want to achieve. You'll need the drive and the energy if you're going to play a bigger game.

Think about how much more you would get done, how your self-confidence would soar which would impact the way you are with the people you meet, the energy you have to play with your kids.

Bottom line is, health serves every other value you have. So even if it isn't a high value to you, take some time to think about the impact it is having on those things in life that you really do value.

Then visualize doing exercise for example, in a way that is aligned with your values. If your core values are the kids, then incorporate them in some way. If spirituality is high on your list then yoga or walking in nature would clearly be aligned to you. If your social life is up there then consider getting out there and joining something like a group Bootcamp or a hockey club where you will meet new people and have social events.

The most important thing to do, is get in touch with the feelings better health would give you and attach it to something that you really do value in life.

Meaningful work

What about your career? Did you give it up when you had kids or are you still doing it in some shape or form? Why is it so important to you? Obviously there is the financial aspect for most of us, but if you are currently supported by a partner then you have to be inspired to do the juggle in a way that makes you want to jump out of bed in the morning with your superwomen hat on. You have to understand your reasons why.

What would it look like according to your values? Look at both the impact it is having on those you love around you by not being engaged in something that is meaningful to you, let's face it, an uninspired you often leads to uninspired kids. Again, don't worry at this stage if you have no idea exactly what you want to be doing, the important thing is to be able to feel what a 'bigger' version of you would be like, to be growing, excited and passionate.

Learning and education

I am ashamed to say that for many years I was seriously deluded by thinking that my 'education' years were over. I had my piece of paper that told the world I had an economics degree, surely that was enough to prove to the world I was a smart cookie? Clearly, I wasn't smart if that was my thinking.

To continue to open your mind through learning and education is one of the most powerful and fulfilling things you can do. These days, it doesn't have to be done in the traditional ways of 'night school' and exams.

In the last two years, I have learnt more about my subject, technology and people than I have in the last 20 years. I can honestly say that it has been exhilarating. Ok, maybe I am exaggerating as learning about technology nearly put me in an asylum but it was necessary!

Your knowledge is your ticket to freedom. I don't mean in an academic sense as quite frankly, I know some frightfully 'intellectual' people, but my god, are they retarded when it comes to basic human behaviour. I am talking about knowledge with purpose, not just the acquisition of information for the sake of looking smart.

We are well and truly into the information age when a large degree of the economy is driven by knowledge. There is a lot of information out there but the real value comes when you have knowledge based on experience.

I could have attempted to write this book when I first started on this journey. I could have spouted a lot of textbook knowledge at you and you would have gained a few insights. But the point is, now that I know what I am talking about because I have been through everything that I am discussing in this book, I can add more value to you. I have, and continue to face, the daily challenges of building a business.

But having said that, you need to educate yourself first in order to put into practice what you are learning, to then be able to offer value to others based on what you truly know.

So what would you love to know about? What would you love to experience in life that you currently don't know how to do? What would you be inspired to read late into the night in order to gain the knowledge to do?

When I first did this exercise, I remained totally blank. The block of all blocks. Once I had got my head around what was important to me, which was a sense of personal success by creating a business that I loved, my family and freedom of time and place, it became simple. I had to educate myself in ways that would make this possible.

So think about what that would be for you? What would you love to know how to do? How would it serve your other values?

Thelma & Louise moments

When was the last time you felt adventurous? Having kids puts a bit of a kibosh on this part of your life for a while, as it is all about the routine (unless you have escaped the norm on this). Well, how about you start to insert a bit of this back into your life?

Your definition would, of course, be different to mine. I would swing towards travelling the world with the kids, extreme sports and learning to dance. You perhaps couldn't think of anything worse! But what is it to you? What would take you out of your comfort zone, yet still be aligned to your values? What would make your heart soar with excitement and trepidation?

The purpose of including this is often we think we need some major life change, and discover 'the thing' that you want to do for the rest of your life. Yet more often than not, you just need a bit more excitement in your life and that can be achieved in many different ways. Get used to stepping out of your comfort zone again but in an enjoyable way. One of the things I am committed to doing this year is heading off in a combie-van with some of my girlfriends. It's not a life threatening adventure, far from it, but it would be something different to how my day-to-day life looks.

Allow your imagination to soar and monitor the feelings you have to allow yourself to dream. You deserve it!

Connection with others

The relationships you have in your life are a bit like your health. Without them, you're nothing. I strongly believe that relationships give the meaning to your life. To have people close to you that you share the ups and challenges in life is priceless. Whether that is family, friends or colleagues, the ability to connect with people on a meaningful level is important.

Ask yourself the question, how connected are you to the people you love and those around you on a daily basis? Crack your relationships and you will 'need' very little else in life.

How is your relationship with your kids? How often do you come down to their level and engage in their world? How much time do you give them that is genuinely all about them. It is so easy as a mother, and I am guilty as hell at times, to be so caught up in what you 'have' to get done around the house, which ends up taking precedence over your kids.

This is one of our drivers for designing our life in such a way that we both work from home most days and we take off a good chunk of time every year. It is now a non-negotiable part of our life because, as parents, we know how caught up we get in everyday life. If we didn't have a pact to eat all together at least 3-4 times a week then it wouldn't happen.

What about with your partner or husband if you have one? Do you communicate in a meaningful way regularly or do you pass each other, too tired to bother to try to find out what they have been up to that day and support with any challenges they may be having? Do you sit down regularly and discuss what you want both individually and together from the year and in five years' time? Do you take the time to create your life together based on what excites you both?

The answer is more often than not, a resounding no because you don't have time. Well you're right you don't have time. Time is running out. Use it wisely.

If you are struggling with relationships visualize how it would be, to be connected to the people you care about, or what it would be like to have a wonderful nurturing relationship with your partner or husband. Try communicating to them in terms of their values and see what happens

But above all, don't forget it is your relationship with yourself that matters. Crack that through personal development work and you will find other relationships will transform. So in this case think about who you want to be in the eyes of others.

Spiritual Connection

Ask me a couple years ago about the desire to have a spiritual connection I would have looked at you somewhat blankly. I have to admit that actually I had no idea what that meant.

I was pretty clear that I wasn't 'religious' in any way, shape or form so surely that had that one sewn up. Ah, what we learn with a bit of knowledge. Clearly through educating myself I have the awareness to understand that it is not a question of whether or not you are 'spiritual'. We are all spiritual beings. The degree to which you harness this aspect of your life will determine how spiritual you are.

If you are currently where I was at with spirituality, i.e. not particularly high on your value set, I would just ask you to at least consider how it would be to understand that you always have the answers you are seeking, if you would just listen to your spiritual self.

Visualise how that would look for you, how would it be to feel like you are being guided at all times by your intuitive self? Your decision-making would suddenly seem a whole lot easier.

Money

The final piece of the puzzle is your financial wealth. On the surface, you will be either motivated by money or not. But the bottom line is you pretty much need money to do everything else you want to do in life.

There are many negative connotations around money; certainly in the UK, it simply isn't British to talk about it. The result? We spend our lives being limited by money and it ends up dictating everything.

What I have come to understand though, is that it is abundant in supply. There is no limit to it, only to what you think you deserve.

Not so long ago I had a reality check. I felt dissatisfied in the area of personal wealth so I did some work around my personal values. I discovered that money didn't feature anywhere even remotely high. No wonder I wasn't earning what I wanted to earn. I went through the process of understanding how more money in my life would serve my highest values, which was a pretty empowering exercise to do. So, for example, if I earned more money I could save more to take the kids travelling for a year, which is one of our goals. If I earned more money I would be able to treat my friends and family more, which I would love to be able to do – you get the picture?

So if you are struggling to come to terms with wanting more money simply think of it in terms of what it would give you. Then understand that you earn money by providing a product or service that fills someone's need.

That said, how would your life look to have an abundant supply of money? What would you do?

"Imagination is more important than knowledge"
Albert Einstein

Go ahead, let go with your imagination, and take yourself back to the 5 year-old self before all your reasoning and belief systems kicked in. This isn't dreaming, it's waking up.

Chapter Four

Do it scared

"Many of our fears are tissue paper thin, and a single courageous step would carry us clear through them."
Brendan Behan

Yeah right. Nice idea, not realistic. I know, I know, suspending disbelief is not a reality and not sustainable. Shame. If it was, the world and its dog would be rockin' and rollin', out there going after their dreams.

There's one stumbling block that kind of puts a kibosh on things.

That ominous thing we call FEAR.

Fear is such a powerful emotion that is responsible for about 98% of the population living half the life they could be.

Your fear may have stopped you doing the last exercise. Could you do it? Could you let everything go and allow your imagination to take over? Did you catch even a glimmer of what is possible for you?

I mentioned in Chapter 1 that identifying my area of strongest dissatisfaction was a pretty emotional experience. What I didn't say was that I was paralysed by fear. It's all very well to realise where you need to grow (and grow up!) in life, but to actually step forth and do something about it brings the emotion to a whole new level.

For days I lay awake in bed at night with two voices vying for my attention. There was one, faint but firm, urging me to step forth and grow. The other was strong and bolshie telling me to crawl back under the duvet and ignore it.

After all everything was 'fine'. Why rock the boat?

The result? I couldn't conjure up any image in my mind about my career. I had so many objections flying at me it was ridiculous.

"I don't have a clue what I want to do"

"I don't have time to fit things into my day as it is"

"I don't know enough about anything to start my own thing"

"I don't have enough experience in anything"

"Anything I do will have to be local and the money wouldn't be worth it"

"I'd have to fit it around my husband's work"

"I wouldn't have a clue about technology now"

Sound remotely familiar? I'm sure you have your own valid reasons for not doing whatever it is your spirit is crying out for you to do. They are perfectly reasonable, all valid, and they are based on your reality so you KNOW they must be true. After all no one else knows how difficult it is for you. In fact I am quite sure that everyone around you would agree with you. That's if you surround yourself with people who are also stuck firmly in their comfort zone, because heaven forbid, that they should start to feel uncomfortable!

But what if the other voice doesn't go away? How do you break through the fear enough to even realise the potential and possibility that exists inside you and then step towards it?

Well, as outlined before, making a committed decision is the first step. Then allow yourself to feel the impact of retreat, indulge in the pain of what could possibly happen if you did choose to ignore it. What would be the impact on your relationships, your kids, your weight, your income, if you did nothing; wallow in the feelings. Ask yourself how mediocre are you prepared for your life to be?

Sounds harsh I know, but it's necessary. To take that first step through the fear you have to be motivated and we tend to be motivated initially by pain, rather than pleasure.

Fear is not going anywhere, however successful you may be. Fear is a part of life. There is no pill that will magic fear away. Every single success story will go hand in hand with a courageous act that involved stepping over fear and every time you grow, you will be faced with it, so the best we can do is try to understand it.

Awareness dissolves illusion and we spend most of our life living under an illusion. Until you have a better understanding of what fear is and where it is coming from it, will dominate your life.

A crash course in breaking the illusion

A while back, I had arranged to meet a mentor and friend of mine, Paul Martinelli in London. I had originally met him in the States as he was running the training, together with Bob Proctor, that I was going through at the time. I was wide-eyed, naïve and excited to be there amongst so many positive people, plus I was thrilled to have 'discovered' what it was that I wanted to dedicate my time to.

Paul had clearly dedicated his life to this work, and he was there with his beautiful wife Kelly. They worked together, driven by passion for what they believed in. He was and still is, an inspiration to whomever he meets. We connected and I was thrilled to hear that he thought I had 'what it took' to make a success of my business I was about to set up.

Fast-forward six months to London, time enough to have ridden the roller coaster of growth. We met for a coffee and we were sitting in a hotel lobby on his brief visit. I skirted around any questions involving me, until he looked me straight in the eye and asked me how it was going. To my utter embarrassment, I dissolved into tears. THIS WAS NOT

ON THE AGENDA! Tears turned to uncontrollable sobbing to snot flying everywhere and every inch of credibility, in my eyes, crumbled right there and then.

Totally un-phased, and being the professional coach that he is, he started to ask me questions.

"What are you so afraid of?" he asked.

Bam! Straight to the heart, no pussyfooting around then!

"I don't know," I muttered, "I just don't think I am good enough."

He continued to probe by asking me what I believed would happen if I was actually successful in this field and what was holding me back. Time after time, he asked me to give him another reason why it couldn't work. After thinking for a while, I would give him answers.

"I don't want to live out of a hotel as a speaker, my kids are too important to me."

"I started coaching and I got lots of clients but every hour of my day was accounted for so I had no flexibility."

I was on a roll now.

"There's absolutely no point in doing any media or PR because I haven't got a website to send them to. I have to concentrate on that first."

On he went, asking the question 'so what else do you believe?' and on I went, racking my brains for reasons to prove myself right, whilst he wrote my answers down. The gaps between my answers grew and I ran out of steam.

He then wrote on the paper:

2 x 2=

2 x 4=

2 x 6=

He asked me to fill in the gaps. I looked at him thinking he had truly lost the plot and promptly answered in two seconds flat.

"So" I asked, "what the hell is that supposed to mean, are you trying to make me feel better by showing me that I know my two times tables because it's not working!"

"My point exactly" he said. "You know the answers to those; you didn't skip a beat in answering. But when I asked you why you couldn't succeed you had to think for a second and the more I asked you, the longer the pause."

"So?" I asked, clearly not getting the point.

"Well, you know your two times table because it is fact. That's why you could answer immediately. When I asked you why you couldn't take your business forward, you kept pausing. Do you know why?"

"No," I said looking more confused by the minute. "I guess I had to make sure what I was saying was right."

Paul looked at me intently and then, very gently said, "It was a good story wasn't it? You made it up. If it was real you would have been able to answer me as quickly as you did with the sums with no sign of thinking about it."

The enormity of what he was saying slowly dawned on me. It was absolutely true. I had crafted a story so convincing that I had convinced myself. Then, right in front of me, he tore it up.

"Now make up a new story" he encouraged, "this time make sure it serves you."

All of a sudden, the conviction I had held for my make believe story felt like it had a slow puncture as the power slowly deflated. Then I saw the truth. We are clever, clever manipulative beings who craft ingenious stories based on our beliefs, and our subconscious mind works tirelessly to protect those beliefs. We see the world through the eyes of our beliefs and our behaviour is subsequently dictated by these same beliefs and as you well know, your behaviour will dictate the results you get in your life.

Does it make them real? No! But this is exactly what we do. Our whole world is an illusion based on what we choose to believe in order to keep us safe. Our subconscious mind is like a protection officer working ferociously to protect our beliefs, doing its best to sabotage any attempts to step beyond them.

The minute you try and plant a new idea in your head such as those formed in the visioning exercise in Chapter 3, you start to physically feel uncomfortable and the most natural reaction in the world is to retreat. Your intellect kicks in to provide you all the reasons why you can't do something, and given they fit perfectly into the story you have crafted you dismiss the idea.

This wasn't always the case though. There was a time before the crafted stories, that you were a natural risk taker, nothing was insurmountable. You went for it, a courageous soul, regardless of spectacular failures. You got up and tried again. As a toddler, you learned to walk and talk, these are no mean feats. As an adult, if you tried to do that you would no doubt give up after the first few falls. You would have crafted a story around why it is too difficult.

"Oh I'm no good at languages, I haven't got an ear for them, I just can't do it."

Well you can speak now can't you? Regardless of the evidence being there that you have the capacity to learn a language, you simply choose not to believe that.

Where do these beliefs come from?

Do you want to know what the scariest thing is? Most of your beliefs didn't even come from you. By age four, before your ability to reason has been formed, around fifty per cent of your conditioning is set. You were a wide-open vessel, susceptible to whatever is being 'fed' to you by well-meaning parents, grandparents, the environment, society and whoever else influenced your life; all contributing to the intricate illusions we have created. These influences continue as you grow, taking the form of teachers, peers and the media all assisting you to conjure up your story about how you can and can't do certain things.

Take some time to think about your parents' beliefs and how you have carried them into your life today (then assess how you talk to your own kids).

In the role of a loving parent we tend to be overprotective by constantly telling our children to 'be careful, you'll fall!' which can influence the degree to which they will take risks in the future, an essential tool to create a fulfilled life. I was watching a video of my kids skiing at Christmas the other day and I realised how much I screamed at my kids to 'TURN' driven by the images in mind of the horrors of what could happen if they just went a metre that way and dropped off the edge of the mountain. That image wasn't even remotely in their mind and highly unlikely to happen. All I was doing was projecting my own fear onto them, potentially slowing down their progress. Having said that they completely ignored me but that isn't to say it hasn't been filed away somewhere in their subconscious mind!

I grew up with extremely loving parents and a particularly risk-averse father. He committed himself to a job for 40 years, which he enjoyed to varying degrees but certainly never loved it. However, to him, it fulfilled his highest values of security and a stable home. I remember several times being told by him that there were 'leaders and followers' in this world and the world needs both. Regardless of whether he actually meant it or not I took it literally to mean that I was destined to be a follower and as a result, I always played the role of a supporter throughout my career 'pre-fish' moment. I never for a moment believed that I could be an entrepreneur with my own vision. Again, simply another story that I had made up in my head that defined my reality for years.

What are your beliefs protecting you from?

There are two common fears that keep us away from our dreams:

1. The fear of success

2. The fear of failure

There are, of course, other fears that you can dress up such as a fear of looking bad, but when it comes down to it they ultimately all fall under these two.

Fear of Success

"Our deepest fear is not that we are inadequate. Our deepest fear is that we are powerful beyond measure. It is our light, not our darkness that most frightens us. We ask ourselves, who am I to be brilliant, gorgeous, talented, fabulous? Actually, who are you not to be?"
Marianne Williamson

You may be surprised to learn that the fear of success is the number one fear.

When you reflect on our society today, it is hardly surprising. Think about when someone succeeds publicly in our society. The initial glory is short lived as the pattern we see time and time again is that people will naturally try to bring successful people in the spotlight down by attaching totally unrealistic expectations on them, resulting in inevitable failure. The media in particular contributes to this belief with the bizarre world of celebrity, dedicating pages and pages to a bit of visible cellulite, the downfall of a sporting hero, or a poorly reviewed film. To many of us, success simply means that a fall that is inevitable will be so much harder so why bother in the first place?

If to succeed means a commitment has to be made by you to continue to succeed, the enormity of the task ahead can seem overwhelming.

Think about someone who sets herself the challenge to loose a significant amount of weight. They succeed and they receive much admiration from the people around them. What then? What happens if they put the weight back on which is quite possible? The disappointment that they would feel in themselves could be too great to bother losing the weight in the first place, and they could feel embarrassed by what other people might think of them if the weight went back on. Subconsciously you know you are going to have to maintain the seemingly hard work forever, with that underlying risk of failure always looming. If you don't put yourself out there in the first place, you won't be seen as a failure in your or other people's eyes.

It is far safer to simply merge into the background and maintain a mediocre existence. Our subconscious mind picks up on this and sabotages any attempt to put you in an unsafe environment.

With success, comes change, and if that isn't a fear that isn't right up, there then I don't know what is. Change comes with uncomfortable feelings and we hate to be uncomfortable. Again, your subconscious mind, in its protective role will do anything to keep you comfortable, which generally comes in the form of behaviour patterns such as procrastination and perfectionism.

 I once went to see a coach because I knew I was procrastinating and my perfectionism was stifling me. She asked me what the benefits were of staying 'stuck' as I was at the time. Given a little time to think, I could identify that it meant I had plenty of time for the kids and I wasn't restricted by any demands on my time. My underlying belief was that if I was in demand in my career then the change in the HK household and the demands on my time would have been far greater. My subconscious mind, in all its wisdom was doing everything it could to keep me right where I was, primarily with procrastination and perfectionism.

Take some time to look back and identify where some of your current beliefs have come from and where perhaps you are afraid of success. Once you realise they are not necessarily your own, you reduce their power.

The Fear of Failure

Half the time we are so wrapped up in what could happen that we become paralysed. In fact, you don't even allow yourself to think big. If you do manage to set yourself a goal then the risk of not succeeding is so great in your mind that you don't go for it in the first place.

If you fear failure, you are likely to attach a lot of meaning to what other people think about you, so fear of rejection and criticism rates highly for you. If you have always been known for being 'good' at things and people think of you in that way then the fear of losing face when you set out to try something new can be crippling.

Interestingly, you will find that many of the world's most successful risk-taking entrepreneurs will have had a past chequered with failures. Many of them were consistently in trouble at school, failed miserably in their exams and yet go on to achieve immense success. Yet the A-grader is held back by their fear of losing face because it has always been expected of them to do well and they are terrified of disappointing both themselves and the people around them.

I have first-hand experience of this and ironically thinking about it as I write, the scenario I just described above, mirrors my husband and I. I worked my butt off at school, achieved pretty much straight 'A's, gained a respectable degree in Economics at a respectable University, and in theory was one of the 'elite'. My husband on the other hand was pretty much kicked out of every school he went to (until he ended up at mine!), he was kicked off his course at University (I mean who on earth manages that?) and finally passed after retakes.

Yet it is he that forged his way through in business first and at any stage, he is prepared to take big risks. He has faced numerous failures and seemingly insurmountable problems yet he refuses to see them that way. To him it is just a question of finding a solution. I always joke with him that he has had to get good at finding solutions as he has got himself into so much trouble over the years (not illegal you'll be pleased to know, well...nothing serious!). But it is absolutely true, that I, however, had always stuck to what I knew I could do. As a result, I am not naturally a solution finder and it has been much harder for me emotionally to step out into the world of business and fail on numerous occasions.

How do you get a grip and step over these fears?

Overcoming fear comes with changing the way you perceive fear and creating new beliefs or in other words, a new story. For the remainder of this chapter I am going to focus on your perception of fear and the following chapter will be focused on creating new beliefs.

Fear is here to stay. You have a choice, embrace it or let it rule you and diminish your life.

Change your perception of fear

I am sure you have heard the term that fear is 'false evidence appearing real'.

Fear is simply a thought, and you know we have the power to choose our thoughts at any given moment. You have to understand that fear is not real; it is simply your perception of fear that is real. Think about when your child calls out in the night or comes to your bedside sobbing because they are afraid there is a monster in the room. To us as a parent, we know that this is all in their mind; there is no real substance behind it. Our fears are the same, they are not real, they simply exist in your mind.

Do it scared!

"Do the thing you are afraid to do, and death of fear is certain"
Ralph Emerson

It is widely known that the best way to overcome your fears is to do the thing you are scared of. Hmm, thanks for that, I hear you say. You have to always keep that in mind though that it's the fastest way to overcome any type of fear. By taking that first action step, you will find that much of the perceived fear will evaporate as you move.

Let people know you are scared if necessary

I found this particularly helpful when I did my first speaking engagement. I was, quite frankly, terrified. Somehow, I had managed to get through life having never stood in front of an audience of people. Quite how I managed that I will never know.

The minute I got on stage looking out to a sea of people I felt my knees go. And I mean seriously go. It was like Shakin' Stevens had taken control of my right leg and was letting rip. One of the first things I said to the audience was an apology if it looked like I was doing a dodgy dance; I had simply lost control of my knee for the time being. Whether or not it was a smart thing to say or not, I don't know, but it diffused the situation for me. It was as though audience was willing me on, and the pressure on me to be perfect, diminished. As a result, the fear dissipated and I can't quite believe I am saying this but I am actually starting to enjoy speaking now. That is quite something coming from a girl that used to literally hide under her mum's skirt when at all possible.

Imagine the worst possible scenario

Our imagination is a powerful tool. We can either use it to imagine all the things that could go wrong in a situation or how things would look if it were to be a success. Obviously the latter is preferable, but if you are struggling to do this then it actually isn't a bad idea to identify what the worst possible scenario could be. When you do this, more often than not, you will realise that the likelihood of it happening is so far fetched it is actually ridiculous. No doubt you will also realise that you are unlikely to 'die' if you get on stage and speak in front of people, or never get a job again if you leave a job to do something you actually enjoy.

Imagine your success

Build a picture in your mind of you doing the thing that you are most scared to do and play the image in your mind often. The more you get emotionally involved in the image, the more you are literally moved to do whatever it is that you are afraid of.

Understand that fear is a sign of growth

If you are experiencing fear, this is simply your mind's way of telling you that you are about to grow and that is a good thing. You only experience fear when you are out of your comfort zone, and when you are out of your comfort zone you generally are about to take some kind of action that is new to you. As discussed in Chapter 1, it is our true nature to grow and therefore you must be on purpose.

If you fail then it is simply a form of feedback

You only actually ever fail in life if you don't learn from your experience and get back up and take what you have learnt and try again. If you can change your perspective to this way of thinking then the act of failing can only ever be seen as a positive and a natural and necessary part of the growth cycle (admittedly this one takes a bit of work).

Keep on swimming…

I have a classic example that incorporates all of the above. I had an irrational fear of learning how to swim front crawl. For some reason as a child, I had never learnt and I had been embarrassed ever since, that I couldn't do it. You see, not only was I an 'A' grader when it came to academics, I was also pretty good at any sport that I turned my hand to. Except swimming. As a result I would avoid the pool, claim I didn't like water for the fear of looking ridiculous in the water.

Not long post 'fish moment' I decided to set myself a goal, get a grip and learn to swim. The fact that I couldn't teach my kids was getting embarrassing. Take note, the pain of not doing became too much. Not only that, but I set myself a goal to be able to swim a kilometre of front crawl within 100 days.

Ugh! It took me days to pluck up the courage to call a swimming teacher and book a lesson. When I finally got in the pool I was officially crap. Any thoughts of me miraculously being able to do it just like that and discovering that the problem was simply that I hadn't tried it before were swiftly put to bed when my teacher asked me to go as far as I could across the pool. I couldn't even do a metre.

A few weeks passed and although I wasn't getting very far it became more comfortable to go to the pool. However, progress was slow and the days were being ticked off too fast for my liking. If I was going to reach my goal then I knew I had to do something fairly radical.

As if by magic, I came across an intensive workshop weekend called Total Immersion. Remember I mentioned that you didn't have to know the 'how'? Well this was one of those classic situations. They just so happened to have space, and it was a rare weekend that I could do. I was so focused on this goal that I blagged my way on as you had to be able to swim a minimum of a length, something I clearly couldn't do, and blagging is quite out of character for me. But, having had a few lessons and gotten over my initial fear I was on a roll.

I turned up for the day, nervous, yet determined to learn. That was until I walked into a room of suspiciously fit looking guys and one other woman. The first thing we had to do was warm up with a couple of lengths. OMG! Seriously, the fear hit me like a tonne of bricks. What do you mean warm up with a few lengths, I could barely do one! Then to my utter horror I discovered that they were filming us.

Still, there was nothing I could do, but go for it. I had made the decision, set myself a goal, committed to the course, and there was no backing out. Was I still afraid? Yes, absolutely, but by committing to something you are compelled to do it. So I did. Badly.

I then discovered that pretty much the rest of the class were training for triathlons and looking to improve their speed. Great. Coming from my world of striving for perfection, I was so far from them it was laughable.

Back to the classroom and one by one they played the video of us. I shrank further and further down in my seat as my time approached with my embarrassment already apparent by my crimson cheeks.

The instructor rested his eyes on me and paused.

"Hmm" he said, "You know I mentioned at the beginning that we have seen all sorts here on these courses and there is nothing that anyone in this room will be doing that we haven't seen before…well, I was wrong."

Oh, lord. Watching the video I realised I was doing a scissor kick / frog's leg type movement that any high jumper would have been proud off, but hardly apt for the kicking required for front crawl.

So in a sense, my worst nightmare in this scenario came true, humiliated in front of a room of buff males and a whole two days still to go. But what I realised quickly was that I didn't die, the world didn't collapse and I got on with it and made it through the weekend. Come the Saturday night I was literally swimming in my sleep, stroke after stroke. I could see myself doing it and by Sunday afternoon after some genius coaching I was swimming. Almost properly.

I went on to proudly achieve my goal on day 82.

I realised that I had wasted 37 years of avoiding the swimming pool like the plague only to discover that all it had taken was a committed decision, taking action and letting go of my perfectionism.

A lesson learnt and it felt good.

The key is to recognise that it is your fear that is stopping you in the first place. I speak to so many people who claim they don't know what they would love to do, and they have genuinely convinced themselves that that is the case, yet when you probe them further you discover they are pretty clear but too fearful to commit to it. It is essential to change your perception of fear and see it as a motivator rather than a reason not to do something. Stepping over that terror barrier will open you up to a whole new world of possibilities!

Chapter Five

You'd better believe it, baby

"Whether you think you can or you can't, you're right"
Henry Ford

Changing your perception of fear is one way to help you move towards clarity and action to become the inspiring woman that is lurking beneath, bursting to come out. But what if there is something going on for you that goes much deeper and no matter how much you want to, you just can't make that move towards what it is that you want? Whether that is discovering what you want to do going forwards, knowing in the back of your mind that your relationships could do with some work, or taking tangible action that you know you need to take, what if you still feel stuck?

Unfortunately, this happens all too often. It's as if your thoughts are detached from your body, no matter how much you think you're going to do something, you don't. I have spoken to so many women who know they have lost their spark, they know they are smart and have something to offer the world AND they want to, yet still they do nothing about it. You can put it down to loss of confidence, self-worth, lack of clarity, or dress it up however you like. I have been the master at this in the past. So the question is, what is really going on?

Fear is generated from your pre-conditioned beliefs, and these make up 'the story' that is your present reality, just like the one that I had made up with Paul sitting in that hotel. In that instance, it was the belief that 'I'm not good enough' that caused the fear in stepping out into the world with my message. These powerful beliefs define you, they define your day, and they define your future. If you could just shift them, your joie de vivre and spirit could be lifted to new levels.

So before we look at how you can identify and change your beliefs, let's get clear on what a belief is. In very simple terms, it is an idea that you are certain about. It's more than an opinion because opinions can be easily swayed. To change a belief you are going to have to have some pretty compelling evidence to change it, but it is possible.

I love how Anthony Robbins describes this. He uses the metaphor of a table whereby the table-top represents an 'idea'. He points out that without legs the table top i.e. the idea, won't stand up to much but if it had legs then the table is a lot more solid. Those legs represent all the evidence from the past that supports this idea and as a result, you are more certain about it. We tend to give meaning to everything and the meaning we give something, turns into a belief. That is why two siblings growing up in the same environment can be subject to the same events and experiences yet they give them different meaning. The meaning they attach defines their future actions and the way they live their life.

Let's take a tangible example to help explain this further. One of my other particularly helpful beliefs (not) that I had for as long as I can remember is that 'I am shy'. Let me tell you I was pretty certain about that one and I had plenty of references in the past to back it up.

I can remember being forever told by family members about how I would hide up my mum's skirts as a child, in fact I can even remember doing it, when anyone tried to talk to me. My school reports in the early years all said that I was painfully shy. Get this one, I was reading my reports the other day at my Dad's house and found one from a particularly unpleasant teacher at my infant school (around aged 5 or 6). Her exact words were:

'Jennie is extremely uncommunicative and very irritating. If I ask her a question then she turns bright red and has even been known to burst into tears!'

How humiliating is that? Even as I write this now I am feeling it; the sensation of feeling so crippled when any attention was directed at me in the classroom. This is a classic example of someone so influential in my life at the time, playing such a big part in solidifying that belief for me. By that point, I was pretty certain I was shy.

Of course I could have chosen not to listen, we always have a choice right? But at that young age, we are so susceptible because our ability to reason has not fully developed. Nope, it was there to stay. I carried it on into my future with an incredible ability to turn red at the slightest thing when attention was directed at me.

As that belief went right to the core of me, my subconscious mind did everything it possibly could to protect me, to keep me safe and away from any situations that require me to speak in front of people. In fact, the truth is I managed to get through school, university and to my mid-thirties without ever having to stand up in front of anyone and speak. Not bad going, huh?

My 'shyness' defined my life. It held me back from so many things. I remember at my wedding thinking I would love to make a speech but I 'knew' that I would be a quivering wreck, go red and probably burst into tears, which would have ruined my make-up, heaven forbid. Actually, on reflection, it was probably a good thing given the length of my husband's speech…they say opposites attract.

As I grew into myself a little more, people began to see me in a different light and yet I would still hear myself say 'I'm shy', I would actually say it out loud. If they disagreed with me I would get defensive because they were questioning a belief I had of myself, I was certain of it and was prepared to defend it.

Did I know this belief wasn't serving me? Yes. The question becomes then, why didn't I do anything about it?

Well, quite simply the pain of getting over my shyness, which in my books would have meant putting myself in excruciating experiences, was far greater than the pain I experienced by believing I was shy. So although I had an idea of things I wanted to be, do and have, this underlying belief would always stop me.

What happens then, if you identify something you want to do that inspires you, in whatever area of life that might be, yet deep down your subconscious is working hard to keep you from it because it would go against the beliefs about yourself?

To move forward, the pain of NOT doing something has to outstrip the pain of doing it. My dissatisfaction of not doing something I loved, in terms of a career, grew so great that I had to discover what it was. When I did, to my horror it meant speaking to people and putting myself in the spotlight. Not only did I have to coach groups of people and stand up and speak, I had to start to see myself as a brand. Imagine the conflict going on there. I tried to cling onto the fact that I couldn't do this because I was shy, yet the thought of not achieving this vision became more and more painful.

I began to realise what it would cost me. Finally a career that I was excited about, but if I held onto this particular belief I would never be able to run a workshop, I would never be able to do a video, I would never be able to speak in public and I would never be able to get my message out to a group of people that I cared greatly about. These were mothers who knew they had lost their spark and were ready to get it back. Then, taking it to an even deeper level, I started to realise that if I didn't follow my dream then what sort of inspiration would I be for my kids?

And so slowly but surely I had to step over my fear and just do it. Every time I took a baby step and didn't get swallowed up by my version of an imaginary monster, the 'table legs' of my belief began to wobble and I started to do things that I never imagined possible.

The bottom line is, your beliefs are simply what you have made certain events that have happened in your life, mean to you. Those meanings that you have adopted are what give you the results in your life because they let you know what, in your world, constitutes pain or pleasure.

That's why so many people avoid personal growth like the plague. Even though they probably know it would be good for them, the pain of doing it in terms of the changes you may be compelled to make, outstrip the pain of continuing to live an uninspired life. Whether they know it or not, their current version of life is in effect a comfortable pain.

It's essential that you get in touch with that real dissatisfaction that you identified in Chapter 1. You've got to let yourself imagine the extreme worse case scenarios of not responding to your dissatisfaction; this is where the power lies. Only then will you start to feel a pain that will motivate you to move positively towards whatever you know in your mind will give you pleasure. It's no coincidence that the women that have the best results with me are the ones that were genuinely dissatisfied. You have to be ready to make the move.

As mothers, there are a few generalised beliefs that seem to go with the role, some of them societal and some of them practical. It's not unusual for a mother to have a strong belief that they are needed to support everyone else in the family.

This was the case with a client of mine who was nearing the time that her youngest child was approaching school age and already that element of silent panic had started to kick for her. What was she going to do? For the past five years she had known that when the kids were both at school she would want to do something else. She couldn't imagine being sat at home busying herself until the school pick up. Financially she didn't really need to work, yet her urge to feel significant in another part of life was getting stronger by the day.

But there was one problem and a major one in her eyes. Her husband worked in the City of London, he left at some ungodly hour and if he was lucky, he might catch the kids before they went to bed. Her belief was that everything would have to be dictated around what he did, she wouldn't get any support and it was virtually impossible for her do anything constructive around school hours. She believed she would always be the one to fully compromise.

Sounds like a pretty realistic belief based on fact, huh? It's one that we could all buy into and probably relate to on a level. The pressures on mothers to perform all the extra 'stuff' is immense, from the school run, school uniform, after school clubs, lunches, birthday parties, you name it we're there and it can be pretty damn overwhelming and quite frankly, exhausting.

We are needed. This is our role. Who the hell is going to do it if we don't? And anyway, we want to, it's what's being a mum is all about.

Now if that is your belief and you are satisfied with that role, then I personally think you are amazing. Seriously, I would love to be you; I would love to embrace it all with daily joy and fulfilment. I'm thinking though, that if you are reading this book then that isn't you either. You may believe that that is how it is for you but alongside that, lays the frustration.

My client fell into the latter category, frustrated but with a core belief that she was needed. I asked her how she knew that her husband wouldn't be supportive and she replied that he hadn't been, to date, and never seemed interested in discussing her frustrations.

After a bit of probing she realised that the way she had approached the subject was to talk about what she potentially would like to do but immediately tell him that she couldn't because he wouldn't be around to help with the kids. Of course, what else could he do but agree, as his work was his reality as well. And so it went on for some time.

I suggested that perhaps if she made a decision to do 'something' even though she didn't know what she wanted to do and then the how would start to work itself out. Until she did that, she would always remain tied to her belief of being 100% needed and as a result be unfulfilled. So, with encouragement she began to explore options.

Her need to work grew and the pain of not doing anything finally outstripped the pain of making a decision to do something. She started working in a florist shop and they gave her school hours so she could work it around the kids. It wasn't long before she remembered exactly how good she was at sales. The confidence started to come back and before she knew it she was adding incredible value to the shop. She began to recognise that her skills were clearly being underutilised and with her newfound energy she moved to work with a private florist. Not only that, she discovered that if she asked, her husband was more than happy to look after the kids on a Saturday if she was working on a wedding. The next thing she knew she was headhunted into a new Spa hotel and landed the job as the Sales and Marketing Manager, working her hours around the kids.

That in its self is inspiring. She made the decision and did it, bit by bit but the magic happened when her belief that she was needed to 100% support her husband and the kids got shaky. She was starting to gain a new perspective as she was managing to do something for herself and keep the house going.

Her husband began to show an interest in what she had been learning and inspired by her, made a decision himself to look at what he really wanted. It then didn't take long for him to work out that the life he was living, despite enjoying his job, didn't meet all his values, one primary value being that he didn't spend enough time with the kids.

Fast forward. He has since left his job of god knows how many years and found something in the same field, yet it allows him to work from home one or two days a week and have more flexibility over his time. He had 3 months off which gave them fantastic family time over the summer and enabled his wife to move forward in what she wanted. Now, back at work he gets to do the school run when he's home and she has been promoted to managing three Spas in a chain. Not bad for a stuck Mum who, although had buckets of value, believed she couldn't do anything significant as she was too needed.

Is life as organised now in their household? No, probably not. Does she still do most things around the house? Yes, but progress is being made bit by bit and as long as she lets go of her own perfectionism, then lunchboxes can go out of the door which have been made by the husband two minutes before the school run.

So, if you have a belief that you have no choice due to your circumstances or environment, then take heart from this scenario. If you would just take the first step then you would be amazed quite how things could turn out. Nothing happens and falls into place overnight, of course not. Change of any degree takes time to bed in.

Knowing your reason 'why'

If you are going to be inspired to continue to take actions that challenge your beliefs you have to have a pretty damn good reason 'why'. You have to be inspired at some level. To start with, you have to feel the pain and that will be your reason why. But at some point, that pain is going to diminish and only being inspired to move towards something that gives you pleasure, will keep you going.

I've known women who were going nuts by feeling like they weren't contributing to the world (remember that's their belief, it isn't real), so driven by this pain, they went out and got a job. Sure, it matched their skill set and got them out of the house but the pleasure was short lived. They weren't particularly inspired by what they were doing and before they knew it they were just as frustrated.

Your reason 'why', is going to be incredibly personal and unique to you. My reason 'why' initially was because I felt so frustrated with feeling the way I did, and it was starting to affect the way I was with my husband and kids. Given that these are the most important things in my life I eventually felt that I had no choice. What is it that keeps me moving forward now though? Well, I have developed a strong sense of purpose with what I want to achieve but I also have a pretty damn exciting vision for my future including things like taking the kids out for a year and travelling, living in different continents and setting up a foundation to support disadvantaged mothers. Once you get emotionally involved in ideas that get you excited and announce them to the world, then there's your drive!

Allow yourself to catch a glimpse of what a smart, sassy women you really are. I don't care what you look like, where you are from, what your dress size is, you are a beautiful, incredibly valuable human being, if you allow yourself to be. This only comes from the inside out though. You have to feel it to believe it.

This is why it is so vitally important that you build inspiring images in your mind of a greater version of you. If you can start to see it in your mind and allow yourself to get emotionally involved in an idea, then it gradually becomes more and more painful to consider that you might never achieve that vision.

The power of your Self Image

We all hold beliefs about the way things are in the world, be it cultural beliefs, beliefs about our role in life or how we should bring up our children. All these shape the way we live our life and the decisions we make. Often by removing ourselves from a certain environment these types of beliefs can be changed.

But those beliefs that lie at the very core of you are the ones that will determine what you will and won't achieve in life. These beliefs make up your self-image, and it's that little sucker that is in charge. You will always act in a way that you believe yourself to be. You will never outperform your self-image.

Maxwell Maltz describes it best in his book Psycho Cybernetics:

"The self-image controls what you can and cannot accomplish, what is difficult and easy for you, even how others respond to you just as certainly and scientifically as a thermostat controls the temperature in your home"
Maxwell Maltz

He goes on to take the example of someone who is trying to lose weight. If that person ultimately has a 'fat' self-image, then no matter how much they try to diet, although they may succeed temporarily they will always find themselves back to what they perceive to be their normal size. It's how they see themselves.

The same applies to people who walk around the place with a victim mentality, always blaming the world for all the unfortunate things that happen to them. They see themselves as a victim and therefore attract circumstances into their life to prove themselves right. Think about my shy example, it was so wrapped up as part of my self-image it drove all my behaviour and therefore results.

Maltz compares it to an airplane that is on autopilot. If, due to turbulence, the plane gets off track, the autopilot kicks in and automatically makes adjustments to bring you back on to being aligned to the pre-programmed route. This is exactly what happens with us, if you start to deviate too much from your self-image an automatic mechanism will bring you straight back on track to creating exactly the same results as you have always created.

Your pain and dissatisfaction will set you off on another path and this is an essential part of the process. But you also have to work hard to change the self-image that you have of yourself if you are going to make any lasting change.

The good news is it is possible to change your self-image. But first things first, you have to identify the beliefs you currently hold.

Get a grip on your beliefs

"An old belief is like an old shoe. We so value its comfort that we fail to notice the hole in it"
Robert Brault

To kick this process off you have to start to do some straight talking and ask yourself honestly, where these beliefs came from. Here are a few questions to get you started:

What beliefs do you have that are both empowering and disempowering about:

- Time

- Money

- Abundance or scarcity

- Relationships

- Your body

- Spirituality

- What you deserve

- What you think you are capable of

- Your current circumstances

- The people you admire

For example, what are your beliefs about money? Do you believe you have to have every academic qualification under the sun to make money? Do you believe you have to work hard for money? Do you believe that money doesn't grow on trees? Or do you believe that money will always come when you need it?

Take it a step further and ask someone to interview you about yourself and record it. You may be surprised at what naturally comes out of your mouth. I imagine is will go something like 'well I'm quite good at this, people tell me this, I am always that, etc.' I find that, when you are talking naturally to someone, the truth comes out.

I have one belief that I know I have to DECIDE to change which is around being late for school. My self-image finds the most incredible ways to sabotage any attempt to get to school on time without having to run the last 100 metres! Although I want to change this, I clearly haven't worked on it enough because I consistently find myself verbalising to the other mums that I am late again, it just comes out of my mouth!

Once you have identified these beliefs, pick out those that you know intuitively are holding you back. Then assess the impact.

Ask yourself:

- What event, experience or person in the past reinforced this belief?

- Do others tell you it's absurd that you believe it to be true?

- Are they actually your beliefs or some you picked up from someone else?

- What have they cost you to date emotionally, physically, financially and in your relationships?

- If you hang onto them, what are they going to cost you going forward?

You may find that once you go through this exercise that you have well and truly grown out of a belief and you are actually holding onto them out of habit. Alternatively, some might seem quite frankly ridiculous now, when you consider where they came from in the first place.

However, there are always going to be the ones that stick with you, despite intellectually knowing that all the evidence suggests they are untrue. What do you do then?

Well, the technique is referred to with a number of words, for example, re-conditioning, re-programming, and affirmations.

I am going to tell it as it is. Pure brainwashing. Everything you have heard about the self-help industry is true; it's all about brainwashing you. I once had a client who was working with me on this aspect and she went home and told her husband about it. He scoffed and claimed that it was all about brainwashing and she came back to me very unsure about the whole thing. That was until I pointed out that wouldn't you rather it was you deciding what to brainwash yourself with, rather than someone else?

You spend your whole life being subjected to subliminal and repetitive messages, and the ones you have chosen to accept, have made you into the person you are today. Every time you engage with media you are subject to an opinion or perspective, whether it is about the state of the economy or how you 'should' look to be considered a sexy, desirable woman. If someone chooses to accept these beliefs, the effects can be far-reaching and devastating. It is no coincidence that so many people are suffering from the economic downturn and there is a frightening rise in the number of people with eating disorders.

What you hear and tell yourself over and over again becomes your reality. Your subconscious mind, which is where your beliefs lie, has absolutely no distinction of what is real and what is not. Therefore, it stands to reason that you have the ability to feed your mind with statements and visions of what you actually want to believe.

I can take my disempowering belief of being shy and flip it on its head to:

"I am confident and outgoing"

It's not enough though, to just say it to yourself. You have to be able to evoke the relevant feelings that you want this statement to mean to you. When I think of myself being outgoing and confident I see myself confidently meeting new people, speaking in front of large groups and engaging in a relaxed way. It comes back to building the picture in your mind of how you want to be. If that means taking inspiration from others that you admire then use that to help you conjure up your own image, but always remembering that you are a unique person and can never be someone else.

Record it, listen to it, write it, create a vision board and look at it every day, whatever it takes for it to become the normal way of being in your subconscious mind, only then will you be compelled to become it.

At the end of the day, the only real way to cement a new belief is to take real tangible action steps that give you evidence of your new belief. I love the saying that you have to 'pray and move your feet' if you want to succeed in life!

Chapter Six

Making it happen

"The big secret in life is that there is no big secret. Whatever your goal, you can get there if you're willing to work"
Oprah Winfrey

This final chapter is all about 'making it happen' and some of the tools and steps that will be essential as you step out of your comfort zone. When I talk about 'it' though, let's be clear. I don't know what you want. I can't tell you what you want. I don't know what inspires you.

But one thing I do know is that somewhere deep inside of you, you know. Your true self, the self that remains when you strip away all the crappy fear and self -doubt knows what your purpose is in life and what inspires you. When you are able to listen and act on this, that's when you know you are 'back'. You jump out of bed in the morning eager to get going, your mind is focused and remarkable things start to happen in your life. Sure, there will still be times when you feel like crawling under the duvet and staying there for the day, but they will be fewer and farther between.

You don't have to be out to conquer the world. You don't have to get fixated on the idea that you have to find the perfect job or business. It might not be that at all for you. Too many people get overwhelmed when they think about doing some kind of self-help that they have to radically change their entire life in some way. It's not so. It's the small changes that make the difference. However, if you really take this work on, then you can't fail to create some pretty radical positive changes, but that comes down the line.

I say think big and start small. I have talked a lot in this book about the power of a big, audacious vision and I stand by that because when you allow yourself to dream you conjure up emotions of desire that have been buried for some time. But if you get stuck in the dreaming, then that is what it will remain, a dream.

The most important thing is that you have to start to move your feet in some way. Even if you don't know what it is that is going to give you your spark back, start with something simple that you really want to do. There is one proviso though; it has to stretch you. That way, you grow.

When I started out, my biggest frustration was my career, but as I didn't know yet what that was going to look like, I stepped out and took on the swimming goal. Totally unrelated to my career (believe me, I wasn't about to become a swimming teacher), but by going for something that was outside my comfort zone it meant I was growing. The very fact that I was doing something that I didn't think I could do was proof to me that I hadn't 'lost it'. It proved that I could conquer personal challenges that didn't revolve around the kids and gave me a sense of personal achievement and satisfaction.

My energy shifted. From being frustrated, stuck, and wallowing in self-pity whilst at the same time telling myself not be so ridiculous because I had a lovely life, I moved into a higher energetic state of being motivated and inspired.

Swimming lessons turned into tennis lessons, which in turn led me to start to educate myself by reading books such as the Inner Game, which is all about the mindset for successful tennis. My research broadened and before I knew it I was thirsty for more and more knowledge. The learning and education area of my life, which had been so stagnant for so long, began to take off. The closest I had come to any kind of educational book since I had kids was 'Up the duff', by Kaz Cooke, a hilarious account of pregnancy!

My enthusiasm began to filter into my social life and my family where I started to discuss what I was learning and before I knew it, I was inspiring other people around me to start to engage a bit more with life. Slowly but surely I realized that I loved it. If I could inspire someone else to get out there and do something in life that has a positive effect on them, no matter how big or small, then I am totally made up. To me it is priceless and makes my heart sing.

And then one day I woke up to this realization. Never before had I been able to say that about anything. I couldn't remember being motivated to study or to invest in myself.

I had my spark back. Opportunities and people started to turn up in my life that I couldn't have imagined pre-fish. I was starting to build connections with people on a global level that I would never have dreamed of.

Take note. I had no idea what 'it' was for me. I had no idea what it was that was going to cause me to be inspired to go beyond my reality at the time. It started with a very poor attempt at swimming across the pool.

So, what about you? What can you start with? What small action could you decide to take today that you know you would love to do but perhaps you have been putting off, due to fear? I had no idea where it was going to take me but regardless, I had faith that as long as I was in action I would be shown the way.

Embrace faith and listen to your intuition

I purposefully haven't touched too much on spirituality in this book for two reasons. Firstly, because it would involve a whole new book and secondly, I am not long into my spiritual journey and it would be wrong for me to portray myself as a seasoned expert.

Having said that, I absolutely believe that having faith is one of the most essential tools you can have when it comes to realising your dreams. Believing that there is a power stronger than you that is supporting you every step of the way is incredibly comforting. The saying 'take a leap of faith' exists for a reason. Sometimes you have to do things without knowing exactly how things are going to turn out for you.

There are many things in this world that we cannot see or explain through our physical senses. It doesn't mean that they don't exist though. You know that, otherwise why would you believe the concept of gravity? You can't see it but you accept it. You can't see oxygen yet you know it is essential for you to survive.

When you really decide to step out of your comfort zone and make a decision to do something bigger than you currently are now, you need to do it hand in hand with faith. You have to learn to trust in what you can't see or understand. As with anything, you are going to come across challenges and at times, they may seem insurmountable. At that point you can either choose to quit or, alternatively, keep the faith that a solution will show itself at the right time. Sometimes faith may be all you have.

There are times when I have been growing my business that I have felt it is all too difficult, too exhausting and too much of a juggle with the kids. Always though, I have had faith that I am meant to be doing this and my faith in the universe and the real voice in my head is what keeps me going when things get tough.

I believe that the universe has a unique purpose and plan for us all. Our job is to discover what that is, as we move through life. Unfortunately, we don't have the birds-eye view and therefore we don't have the whole picture. So when events happen in life that are inexplicable, we start to question any kind of faith we may have. But what if you are supposed to take everything you have learnt from life to date, or specific incidents, and use them to add value to the world? Let's face it; I have managed to write a whole book here based on the premise of me throwing a fish at my husband's head. It's ridiculous in isolation, yet I have learnt so much as a result, that I am able to add value to women feeling the same frustrations.

You have been blessed with an incredible faculty called intuition. Intuition can come in different forms such as 'hunches', a gut feeling, or could even be delivered in a dream. You will have experienced flashes of inspiration before, however big, small or seemingly banal. Your intuition tells you what you need to hear at that very moment.

If you have read the book Eat, Pray, Love by Fiona Gilbert you may recall the first scene, which finds her having a melt down on the bathroom floor about what to do about her marriage and for the first time in her life, she prays for a message from God or if you prefer, the universe. She receives her message:

"Go back to bed Liz."

Hardly ground breaking, but exactly what she needed to do in that moment.

Your level of faith is dependent on how prepared you are to open up and listen to your intuition, and more importantly act on it, when perhaps the advice doesn't make sense to you or it isn't what you want to hear.

There are many people in this world that have developed their intuition so far that they are able, at any moment of the day to ask the universe a question and receive an answer. In fact, I would go as far as to say that all of the most successful people in this world use their intuition regularly to make decisions.

Wouldn't that be amazing? Imagine being able to ask the right questions and get the answers coming back to you and you have enough faith in those answers, that you take inspired action.

Intuition is not something that is handed out to some particularly gifted people in the world. We all have access to it, it really just depends how open you are to it. The sad thing is, as a child you were incredibly intuitive, but unfortunately over time you learnt to listen more to those external to you; your parents, your teachers, your peer group and little by little, you began to doubt your intuition and shut down this channel of information.

You became a much more rational 'thinking' being and certainly what I found when I was searching for clarity, was that I was forever stuck in my head. In fact, I would end up going round and round in my head trying to work everything out. It literally hurt.

What you need to do is get back to your heart. Listen to what your heart is telling you because it is at this level that we connect with the universe.

Sometimes your answers will come when you least expect it, so you have to be able to recognize different things as signs, and you have to be prepared to investigate even when it doesn't make sense. Let me give you an example of what I mean. A close friend of mine had, for some time, been trying to source a low cost way of producing some branded stationery.

She had been going round and round in circles for weeks. She and I often chat about this sort of thing as her business was born out of this work, so it was no surprise that she rang me in excitement one day. She said:

"Jen! I have discovered the perfect supplier."

So I asked how it had come about.

"I asked the universe!" she replied.

That night as she went to bed she asked the universe specifically where she could find what she was looking for. She had a bizarre dream but remembers waking up thinking of one word that had come out of the dream that she just knew she had to remember. She had no idea what that word meant but her intuition was telling her that it was important. She searched the word on Google that morning and it turned out to be a bespoke greeting card company. On investigation, she discovered who their suppliers were and bam! They were exactly what she was looking for.

Could she have ignored this word and brushed it off? Yes of course, but due to her understanding and faith in the universe delivering, she now has clarity on an important part of her business.

You may well receive flashes of inspiration about what you could possibly do in an area of your life where you are experiencing dissatisfaction. When this happens, whether you dismiss it or not, you need to know that it is achievable by you otherwise it wouldn't have come into your head. If you can see the idea on the screen of your mind then it is possible for you to achieve it. Remember, don't discount anything that comes into your head on the basis that you don't know the 'how' yet.

Practice Gratitude

Have you ever noticed that when you are feeling good about life in general, good things tend to happen? On the other hand if you start the day by yelling at the kids and spilling your coffee then things tend to go downhill after that and you can't seem to shift it. Sometimes this can last for a short period of time but it can also last for days, months or even years for some people.

I have already mentioned that we attract into our lives whatever is in harmony with the way we are thinking. The trick is obviously to maintain a positive mindset. Clearly life gets in the way though at times, making this a challenge.

One of the most powerful ways to keep yourself in a positive mindset is through practicing gratitude. When you take the time to really feel grateful for what you have in your life, then you will instantly experience a shift in the way you are feeling.

It doesn't matter what is going on in your life, you can always find something to be grateful for. Having a roof over your head, or having the use of your eyesight to see the world in its beauty, the friendships you have and your adorable children, or simply being able to make yourself a cup of tea in the morning. It sounds so simple yet it is very powerful in shifting your moods.

If you can make it a habit to start your day from a place of gratitude by physically writing down at least five things you are grateful for and really feeling it, then I think you will be surprised how much calmer and positive your day will begin.

By setting yourself up for the day like this, you will find you move much quicker towards your goals than you could imagine.

Surround yourself with 'yes' people

The people you spend your time with can be the make or break of you. Did you know that you are the sum of the five people you spend most time with? It's totally natural as like attracts like.

Think about the friends you have. Are they all real friends? Do you look forward to conversations you have with them and come away inspired? Or do they zap your energy and you come away drained? How many people do you know that spend their days bitching about life and how difficult things are? If you have people like that in your life, be warned. The minute you start to attempt to share your new vision they will more than likely slam you down. People see themselves in other people, and it is likely that any change on your behalf will provoke a questioning in their own minds about their own insecurities. Some will rise to the challenge, and some will react negatively, which could influence you.

It is so important to get out there and find your 'yes' people. These are the people that are going to be championing you, supporting you, and importantly, believing in you. If you don't feel like you have these people in your life, you have to go out and find them. There is something like seven billion people in the world; they are out there waiting for you!

I have found it very beneficial to mix in circles where people are further up the path than me, as my visions are perfectly normal to them. They never question whether my visions are possible; they simply encourage me to go for it, often hand in hand with great advice along the way. A good example of this is when we spend time in Western Australia.

For those couple of months a year I am surrounded by high achievers and one of those areas of achievements is health and fitness. Everywhere I look, there are toned, bronzed, fresh-faced people. All my friends and family out there fall into that category. They place a huge priority on their health; triathlons are perfectly normal, ridiculous swims are perfectly normal, getting up at 5am to exercise is perfectly normal. And what happens whenever I am there? My level of fitness skyrockets. I am there pounding the streets, sprinting on the beach, out in the pool (because I can now!) but very quickly it becomes a way of life. And why? Because I am surrounded by people doing this and I feed off their motivation. I am fairly motivated in this sense, but without doubt it goes up a notch every year we go.

One of the most powerful things you can do is to join, or set up your own mastermind group. A mastermind group is when a group of likeminded individuals come together on a regular basis to support and brainstorm each other's ideas and challenges. The power of the collective mind, if carried out in a focused manner, can be one of the most effective ways of generating new ideas and overcoming challenges. Again, where possible make sure you are one of the least advanced in the group, as that way you will be stretched to achieve. Your vision could already be their reality making it seem much more attainable.

Get a mentor or a coach

Every successful person in life or business will have some kind of mentor, paid or not. Mentors guide, help and nurture you. You will probably have had various mentors at different times in life, whether they have been family members, friends, or someone in your career.

Finding the right mentor has become much easier now with the emergence of social media. In whatever area of life or business you are looking to expand into, whether it is to improve your health, your fitness, your spirituality or your career there are fantastic mentors out there dedicated to helping you grow. I would recommend finding someone in your field that has been there, done that, and had success that is worthy of what you want to achieve. Don't be afraid to hang out in their space for a while, whether that is online or offline so that you can get a feel for the way they work, the way they communicate and intuitively you will know if you will connect with them which is really important. I have made the mistake before of going for mentors simply because they are at the top of their game, yet when it came down to it the connection simply wasn't there. Our values weren't aligned therefore there was little understanding between us.

You should always be prepared to pay for a mentor or coach if you expect to get the best out of them. Good mentors are mentoring for the right reasons, i.e. their desire to help people grow and succeed, but there is no reason why they should be giving their precious time away for free. If you are not prepared to invest in them, then how can you possibly expect them to invest in you?

Then, once you find the right mentor, do what they say! They have been there, got first-hand experience and if you have the right mentor they will have already succeeded in what you are trying to achieve, so you can pretty much guarantee they have good perspective and know what it takes to succeed.

Along the way you may find that they give you negative feedback, it is their job to be honest not nice. Take it for what it is; it's simply feedback. Don't take it as a personal assault; they are doing their job to get the best out of you. At the same time, you have to be open and honest with them, as they can't be expected to read your mind. Let them hold you accountable, it's their job. If you are not holding yourself accountable you can be sure that no one else is, as people don't have the headspace or time unless it is their specific role.

You have to be willing to do what it takes

To achieve anything in life you have to be prepared to do what it takes, and often that means giving up something of lesser value.

When I started to study human potential, you would find me pretty much every night at my desk studying. I literally spent hours and in fact, I still do put in the hours every week. This meant other things took a back seat, as there simply wasn't enough time in the day to do it all. Reality TV went out the window (although sadly I have to admit, X-Factor still gets a look in!). And I have always been renowned for falling asleep on the sofa, and yet now you can regularly find me up late and energised to learn.

Look at what you do in a day and it will tell you your hierarchy of values. If these aren't serving you in reaching your goals, then it may be time to make an adjustment. More often than not though, if you are genuinely on purpose you will find that this happens naturally. As you align yourself more and more with these values, you will find that people and activities in your life that don't fit with them will drop away, and it is important to let them. I know I went through a stage of wanting to hold onto friendships that I had had for years but when I actually thought about it, I realised we no longer had anything in common. I was a different person, as were they, and unless you have some kind of deeper connection, then understand that some relationships no longer serve either of you. You'll be doing both of you a favour.

Value yourself enough to invest in yourself

If there is one thing I have learnt over the past couple of years, it is that you are the most important factor in your growth. No one else can do it for you. You may have the best family, the best friends, the best mentors that money can buy, but if you are not investing in yourself to be the best you can be, then it won't be long before you slip back into your existing ways. You can't control anything else in this world apart from you. You are your most valuable asset.

I would say the past couple of years have been quite a roller coaster for me. When I look back now, I can literally map out when I have been focusing on developing myself and when I haven't. There is no surprise, that when I let it go for a period and focused more on the marketing and business side of things to the exclusion of working on myself, there would be more of a downturn in how I was feeling and handling life if general.

Listen up, especially you British gals out there. Personal growth is not some weird American thing where you have to whoop around the room hugging everyone in sight. It is the core ingredient to every successful person that I have come across. They all embrace it. Too many people I know won't go near it because it smacks of a label saying that you 'need' it. That is crap. Nobody needs it, but if you are keen to make some positive changes in your life then you would be incredibly naive not to embrace it in some way. There are so many different approaches out there and I can pretty much guarantee that there is one that would suit you. There are also many different teachers and again, if you took the time to look you would find someone that you resonate with.

As mums, unfortunately at times we have a habit of putting our needs last and the thought of investing in yourself other than a new pair of jeans from time to time can be so far from your mind, it is ridiculous. This is your time! You have so much to give, so much to learn, so much more to experience. It starts with giving yourself permission and actually, that is all personal growth is about.

Take the time out to work out what it is that you really want and then invest in yourself to make it happen, whether that is training, studying, personal trainers, you name it, there is something and someone out there that can show you exactly how to do what you want to do. With the emergence of the internet, you can pretty much do it all from a laptop in the comfort of your own home if you want to.

You have to be prepared to ask for help. I am constantly amazed at how many people, when pressed, have a good idea about some of the things they would love to do but have never verbalized it, simply because they haven't got a clue how to achieve it. Most people are afraid to ask for help and, as a consequence of trying to do everything alone, nothing gets off the ground. I am not suggesting you go around shouting from the rooftops to everyone you meet but be aware just how connected people are these days.

What to do when everything seems to be going pear shaped

When I make up my mind about something, I want it now, in a stamp-my-feet kind of way. Once I had a clear idea of what I wanted to do as a career after a long period of no clarity, I had a child-like expectation that it would all happen overnight. Hmm, I soon got that one knocked out of me.

Of course, it never works like that. If you have set yourself a big enough goal, believe me, chaos will follow at some point and then at many points after that. You will be tested to the limit as to whether you continue on your quest or quit. That's when it is vital to understand the growth cycle.

I recall a time when I was that close to jacking it all in. I knew what I wanted to achieve in business and yet it wasn't happening fast enough for me, in fact, it didn't appear to be happening at all. Thankfully I had the sense to have a personal coach and she very gently reminded me that I was simply on the journey of growth and where I was right then, was exactly where I was supposed to be and what I would learn in this period would, in time, be of huge value to both me and future clients.

Growth is not always pretty. Let's take a real tangible example of growth and the chaos that ensues before it. You get pregnant and assuming it was your aim to get pregnant in the first place, you experience an incredible elation, which turns swiftly into shock, and then in my case was immediately followed by the utter terror of 'oh my god what the hell have I done' type feeling.

Then the sickness kicks in and life takes a nosedive. The days are endless, you are knackered by breakfast time, the nausea is a killer and you can't see an end to it. Then things progress, the baby grows, you grow literally, and if you are lucky you move into the part of the process when you are blooming (well actually I would like to caveat that, I am not sure I did, but that is what all the books tell you anyway).

You go through a period of blissful ignorance, or denial as I did, feeling the wonderment of your baby kicking inside and you coast along getting fat and happy. Until before you know it, you have reached the next part of the cycle. The realisation hits that OMG you have to get this thing out of you. You have no idea how you are going to achieve that and the fear kicks in. The big day finally arrives and my god the terror and the pain that follows. But the point is, you have no choice. This is what it takes to achieve your dream of having a child.

It's absolutely no different to giving birth to an idea, a big goal, a business or even your purpose. There are going to be times of elation, there are going to be times of steady growth when things are feeling good, and there are going to be times when you are terrified of taking the next step or you are beyond frustration because you don't know 'how' or 'what' you should be doing. And the good news is this feeling often comes just before a big shift. That is, if you are committed to moving forward.

But can you see? If you relate it back to the childbirth example, they are all absolutely necessary parts of the cycle. You can't produce a bouncing baby without going through these cycles. You can't create a life that you love or a successful business without going through these cycles of chaos – it is simply part of it.

And does it stop when the baby is born? No! It gets 10 times worse! You feel helpless, vulnerable and insecure at times. No one ever taught you to be a parent and the sleepless nights are necessary, they are an essential part of the growth of the baby and your development. Will it stop when you reach a certain level of growth? No! It won't because you will always come up against new challenges. It's part and parcel of growth.

Being aware of this cycle upfront allows you to accept and dig in when times are tough. Everything in this universe is in perfect balance, you will never have pain without an equal and opposite gain, but you just may not be able to see it at the time.

Growth isn't supposed to be easy, otherwise everyone would do it and let's be honest, a high proportion of the population doesn't engage in it. Growth takes understanding, it takes desire, but above all, it takes persistence. Knowing that wherever you are right now in the growth cycle is exactly where you are supposed to be. Awareness of this may well be the one thing that will prevent you from quitting in a chaotic stage.

I hope I haven't freaked you out in this chapter with honesty about the journey ahead. Some people prefer to operate in complete ignorance but I wish I had been a little more prepared when I woke up and stepped into the role of creating my life. I feel there are way too many people out there selling the dream to people with no mention of what it takes. Bottom line is, it takes hard work, but if your reason 'why' is big enough, then you will do what it takes and embrace the ride.

Final thoughts

If you have made it this far through this book, then a big high five to you. You are in the few percentage of people that ever finish a non-fiction book, and more important than that, you have taken a first big step towards stepping into your potential that is begging to be fulfilled.

Think of this book as a process that you can now take away and implement. Firstly, identify where your greatest dissatisfaction lies, feel the impact, take responsibility for where you are at right now and then make a decision to make some changes moving forward. To do that, you have to create your vision by asking yourself if you didn't believe it was impossible what would you love to be, do and have? Get emotionally involved, connect to your reason why and start to move your feet.

You will only progress if you learn to embrace and move through the fear that you will inevitably come up against if you have set your sights high enough to stretch you and you may well have to change some of your existing beliefs along the way.

It's then all about the journey. I laugh when I say that now, as a friend of mine constantly mocks that saying but as clichéd as it is, you can't get away from it. Your experience and success moving forward will be dependent on the people you surround yourself with and your attitude to growth. If you wait around waiting for all the pieces of the puzzle to fall into place then believe me, you will be sitting there, just as frustrated this time next year - in fact let's be honest, even more frustrated. You will never have all the resources you need at your disposal, the childcare sorted, the money to invest in yourself, the perfect idea, the right gym equipment, whatever it is that is currently your excuse and is holding you back. But somehow, the how's will reveal themselves with every action step you take.

Just decide and start. Remember, any inspired thought that comes into your mind can be done. Focus on what you perceive to be missing in your life right now and you will find, as you start to move, that every other part of your life will expand further.

But more important than anything, give yourself time to stop and listen. Cut the noise, cut out the piles of washing, cut out the endless 'to do' list for just ten minutes a day and be still in your mind.

That is where the magic happens and your answer to your passion, purpose and identity lie.

It leaves me to say thank you for allowing me to share this journey with you. I hope the stories and principles in this book have inspired you in some way to live with passion and be all that you can be.

I'd like to get to know you…

If this book has struck a chord with you and you would like to keep in touch then please do head over to my website at:

www.jenniehk.com

where you will find a free report on the 7 reasons why you're not doing what you really could be right now and a 7 day challenge that will get you started!

I look forward to connecting with you.

Love

Jennie x

Bibliography

Gilbert, Elizabeth. *Eat Pray Love, One woman's search for everything*. Bloomsbury Publishing, London, New York, Berlin, 2006

Maltz, Maxwell. *The New Pyscho-Cybernetics. The Original Science of Self-Improvement and Success That Has Changed the Lives of 30 Million People* (edited by Dan S Kennedy & The Maxwell Maltz Foundation). Penguin Publishing, USA, 2002.

Lightning Source UK Ltd.
Milton Keynes UK
UKOW07f1409021214

242531UK00009B/586/P